D0006363

MARK OESTREICHER
SCOTT RUBIN

::MY
CHANGES

MS+CHG
MIDDLE SCHOOL SURVIVAL SERIES

 **ZONDERVAN®**

ZONDERVAN.com/
AUTHORTRACKER
follow your favorite authors

 in:vert

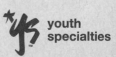 youth
specialties

My Changes
Copyright 2008 by Mark Oestreicher and Scott Rubin

Youth Specialties products, 300 S. Pierce St., El Cajon, CA 92020 are published by
Zondervan, 5300 Patterson Ave. SE, Grand Rapids, MI 49530.

ISBN 978-0-310-27883-2

Cover design by Gearbox
Interior design by Mark Novelli, IMAGO MEDIA

Printed in the United States of America

08 09 10 11 12 • 20 19 18 17 16 15 14 13 12 11 10 9 8 7 6 5 4 3 2 1

DEDICATION

Scott wants to dedicate this book to the small group of junior highers that he and his wife, Lynette, lead—the self-designated "Flying Squirrels": Matt, Davy, Cal, Zach, Scott, Kayla, Ashley, Erin, Tanner, and Connor. You really *are* influencers!

Marko has already dedicated his books to most everyone he knows, so he dedicates this one to the Flying Squirrels, too!

THE FLYING SQUIRRELS

■■ CONTENTS

SECTION 6: FAITH CHANGES

SECTION 7: RELATIONSHIP CHANGES

SECTION 8: DIFFERENCES BETWEEN GIRLS AND GUYS

SECTION 9: QUESTIONS GIRLS ASK ABOUT GUYS

SECTION 10: QUESTIONS GUYS ASK ABOUT GIRLS

ACKNOWLEDGMENTS

Scott wants to thank Lynette, Tanner, Dawson, and Brock—thanks for the jump hugs that keep me going. Thanks also to all the volunteers at Elevate who show up week after week to follow Jesus with middle schoolers! Thanks to my mom and dad, Howard and Carolyn, for not strangling me when my own junior high changes were making you crazy. And thanks to God, for loving me.

Marko thanks Jeannie, Liesl, and Max—simply the coolest family in the entire universe. YS publishing team—thanks for humoring me with these books over and over again and for your always excellent work. Thanks to my friends in middle school ministry (like Scott!) who've helped me think through these issues about early adolescent development.

INTRODUCTION

See this really dorky picture right here? That's me, Marko, when I was in middle school. Nice shirt collar, huh? Can you tell I wasn't the most popular kid in school? Uh, yeah.

How about this groovy picture? That's me, Scott, back during my middle school years. That haircut *rocked*, huh? Sure, whatever.

We wanted you to see those pictures—as embarrassing as they are—because we want you to know that we remember what it's like to be a middle school student. Partly, we remember because we've been working with middle schoolers in churches for a long time. We don't work with high school kids or with any other age group. That's because we're both convinced of a few things:

- First, middle schoolers are the coolest people in the world. Really! We'd rather hang out with a group of middle school students than any other age group.

- Next, God really cares (we mean, *REALLY CARES*) about middle school students—about you. And we believe God is stoked about the possibility of having a close relationship with you.

- Finally, the middle school years (from about 11 to 14 years old) are HUGELY important in building a FAITH that will last for your whole life.

This book is the fifth in a new series: The Middle School Survival Series. The first book is all about your faith (that's why it's called *My Faith*—duh!). The second book is about your family (it's called, not so surprisingly, *My Family*). The third book is about you and your friends (it's called *My Friends*). The fourth book is all about school—it's called *My School*. And the sixth and final book is also out now. It's all about your future. (We bet you can guess the title—that's right, *My Future*.) We hope you'll read them all!

Oh, one more thing: You don't have to read these 75 "chapters" in any particular order. It's not that kind of book. You *can* read them in order if you want (if you're one of those people who likes order); or you can just flip through and read whatever catches your attention.

We believe in you, and we'll be praying for you (really, we will) that while you read this, you'll grow in your understanding of God (just like the Bible says Jesus did when he was your age), of how much God loves you, and of how God would do anything to let you know him.

Marko and Scott

1. THE DIFFICULTY OF NAMING THIS BOOK

There are five other books in the Middle School Survival Series (*My Faith, My Family, My Friends, My School,* and *My Future*). Once we'd decided on the topics for those five books, their titles were really obvious. So we never talked much about any of them.

But the title of this book—*My Changes*—was a real challenge. We knew we wanted to write a book about all the changes you're experiencing in life. (Did you know that other than the first two years of life, people experience more changes during their middle school years than at any other time in their lives?) So we were sure the book would be about changes; we were just concerned that the title "My Changes" sounded dorky.

So we considered a few dozen other ones. Here are some of them, just to give you an idea of what we talked about:

My Body: Nope, the changes you're going through aren't just about your body. And we really didn't want this to sound like a sex book that your mom would buy and leave on your pillow as a special "gift" for you.

My Transformation: For a while we thought this title had potential because you really are going through a transformation—a complete change. But then we thought the word was just too long.

My Growth: Sounds like something you'd ask a doctor to remove.

My Development: Nah. That sounds more like a schoolbook to us.

My Transition: This wasn't a bad idea. We just weren't sure anyone would know what it meant until *after* they'd read the book!

My Puberty: We never seriously considered this one, but people kept suggesting it. We just couldn't picture any middle school student wanting to read a book with that title.

So *My Changes* it is—like it or not. In the end, this title really does describe what this book is about.

If you're in the beginning of your middle school years, this book will give you a massive "heads up" to the stuff you're about to go through in the next couple of years. If you're at the tail end of your middle school years, then we hope you'll find that this book describes a bunch of the changes you've been experiencing and talks about them in a way that helps you understand them better.

SECTION 1

ON-RAMP
TO CHANGE

2. EVERYTHING'S CHANGING

There are really only two times in life when everything changes.

When you were born (awwww—we bet you were cute!), your little body and brain went through massive changes for a couple of years. Think of the difference between a newborn infant and a two-year-old. The newborn can't do anything but eat (with help), sleep, cry, and fill a diaper (with the occasional cute gurgle thrown in). But by two years old, they're miniature walking, talking, toy-wrecking wonders.

The other massive time of change? You're soaking in it. Or you're about to enter it. Or you've just gone through it.

You've probably heard this word: *puberty.* It's not just about sexuality and stuff. It's the word to describe a short period of time, usually during the middle school years, when your body and mind kick into high gear, changing, morphing, shifting, becoming less like a kid and more like an adult.

And it's often a bit freaky.

Your body's changing. Your brain is changing. Your emotions are changing. Your friendships are changing. Your relationship with your parents is changing. Your faith is changing.

Really, this is the reason we (Marko and Scott) totally dig working with middle schoolers. We *love* helping students understand all these changes and how cool it all is (or can be).

If you're feeling a bit weird these days, it's probably because of all these changes. That's why we wrote this book (to help you understand all that stuff), and we hope that's why you're reading it.

3. THIS IS GOOD—IT'S GOD'S PLAN FOR YOU

We have two promises for you: one good, one not so good.

Let's start with the not-so-good promise. We promise you that sometimes, probably a whole bunch of times (maybe even all the time), you're going to feel lousy during your middle school years. You're going to feel like the changes you're going through stink. You're going to feel like something is just off and wrong with your body. You're going to feel really frustrated with how easily you feel frustrated.

Newsflash: That's normal. In fact (here comes a big secret—ready?), we (Marko and Scott) aren't really all that smart; we can only make that promise about how lousy you're going to feel at times because *every* middle school student feels that way from time to time.

Here's the other promise, the good one: We promise that all this change is a good thing. Here's how we know it's good: God invented it. That's right. It's not like God stood back at the end of creation and said, "Ah, my creation is very good—except for those middle school years. I kinda messed them up."

No, God's creation is *always* good. And God designed this time and process of change so that you could grow to a place where you can really experience life to the fullest. See? That's God's loving motivation for all this messy change stuff.

So why is it such a pain? Well, truly deep change is usually difficult and messy. Otherwise it wouldn't be truly deep change; it would only be surface-level change.

Have you ever seen a chick come out of an egg or a butterfly come out of a cocoon? In both cases they have to work like crazy. But if you help them, then they probably won't live. They *have to* go through the hard work—it's part of what makes them strong enough for the next part of their lives.

The same is true for you. The changes you're going through can be really difficult and annoying and not a lot of fun to experience. But these changes are preparing you for the rest of your life.

4. WHY IS THIS HAPPENING?

Can you picture us showing you an old-school film right now, in black and white, with some dude wearing a dorky suit and standing at a chalkboard with an outline of a boy and a girl? He'd say, in a deep voice, "Change. You're really changing a lot, aren't you? Let's take a deeper look at these changes and try to understand *why* all this is happening."

Uh, yeah. We don't have that movie. And you wouldn't want to watch it if we did.

But the question is a good one. *Why?* Why is all this happening to you?

The answer is both simple and not so simple.

The simple answer: All this change is happening to you because you're growing up. Duh!

Now for the not-so-simple answer. Really, you've been changing every minute of every day for your entire life. And you'll continue changing every minute of every day for the rest of your life. Things grow, things get stronger or saggier, thoughts and emotions develop or fade.

But what's unique about your middle school years is the massive quantity of change. If a normal amount of change for a human is like walking up a tiny little hill, then your changes are like climbing a 10,000-foot mountain. Blindfolded. Without any equipment. Or any clothes.

Okay, maybe we exaggerated a bit. But you get the idea.

We don't really know why God planned for young teenagers to have *all* these changes *all* at once (rather than a little bit at a time, over a longer period of years). But we *do know* that if you didn't go through all the changes we talk about in this book, then you'd have a not-so-great life as an adult. Really! If you lived as an adult with the body, mind, faith, and emotions of a little kid, then your life wouldn't be the "full life" that Jesus talks about in John 10:10:

> I HAVE COME THAT THEY [I.E., YOU!] MAY HAVE LIFE,
> AND HAVE IT TO THE FULL.

THAT'S what this change is all about!

5. A LITTLE HISTORY

Here's something strange that you might not know: The word *teenager* was never used until *fewer than* 100 years ago. The more formal word for the teenage years—*adolescence*—was invented just after 1900. That might sound like a long time ago, but it's a pretty short time when you consider how long humans have been around.

In fact, hundreds of years ago there was no such thing as the teenage years. Kids were kids, and then they were considered young adults. Every culture around the world used to have these things called "rites of passage." They're ceremonies or tasks that people your age went through in order to be considered an adult.

But about 100 years ago, our culture started to change. We started to understand the importance of education beyond elementary school, and high schools started to pop up. (They weren't required until a little more than 50 to 60 years ago.) And at the same time, our culture started to create some space for teenagers to be teenagers instead of rushing them into adult responsibilities.

At first, the teenage years were viewed as a couple of years long, around the 15th or 16th year. Then, when high school became required, people started thinking of the teenage years as being from 13 to 18 years old.

With those societal changes, teenagers started creating their own culture—their own clothing styles, language and slang, music choices, and stuff like that.

There are still changes taking place in all this cultural stuff. Like, when we were in middle school, the things we were exposed to were probably a lot closer to what you experienced in fifth or sixth grade. And these days, most experts would say the teenage years are about 10 to 15 years long, from about 10 or 11 years old to the mid-20s.

So when your grandparents, or even your parents, talk about how different things are for teenagers today from when *they* were your age—they're right!

6. WHAT ARE THE TEENAGE YEARS ABOUT?

Okay, make sure your seatbelt is fastened tight because we're going to teach you three big words in this little chapter. (You can use them to impress your parents and teachers.)

People who study teenagers (like, college professors who specialize in understanding teenagers) talk about the teenage years as being a period of time between childhood and adulthood. And they say there are three "tasks" of the teenage years—not tasks like taking out the trash or finishing your homework, but three things teenagers must try to figure out related to who they are before they become adults.

The first one is **Identity**. Your identity is who you are or who you *think* you are. We know that's kind of hard to think about. It's especially difficult to think about when you're a young teenager because your brain is barely able to handle thoughts like that. In a few more years, this will be a bit easier for you. Just know that your identity is how you think about yourself. It's the sum total of all the conclusions you make about yourself, who you are, and why you exist.

The second task is called **Autonomy**. That's a big word that just means "being unique" or "being different." As a teenager your task is to figure out how you're different from other people. It's about discovering if you and your choices really matter.

It's wrestling with the question: *Why should I be responsible?*

And the final task is **Affinity**. (These aren't in any order, by the way—you'll work on all of them at the same time for lots of years.) *Affinity* is a fancy word for things that are alike. So this task is about figuring out where you belong, where you fit. Little kids fit into their family. Adults fit into a certain community or group of people. Where do *you* fit? Where do *you* belong?

We're not suggesting you sit down with a pad of paper and write answers to these questions. It doesn't work that way. You have to live with the questions for a number of years. You have to try things on (almost like trying on clothes before you buy them). You have to make some bad decisions and learn from them. You have to experience success and failure.

7. OTHERS' EXPECTATIONS

One of the major differences of being a teenager (from what things were like when you were a little kid) is what people expect from you. You've probably already noticed this.

When you were a little kid, people had pretty simple expectations, like:

- Listen when you're being spoken to.

- Eat your vegetables.

- Be respectful to your parents and other adults.

- Don't lie.

- Cover your mouth and nose when you sneeze.

And other things that don't take too much work to figure out.

But now that you're a teenager, this really begins to change. Adults will start (they've probably already started) treating you like a "junior adult." This can be frustrating at times because you won't always like being treated like a "junior." But it can also be pretty cool because it's fun to realize you're on the road to adulthood:

- Adults will expect you to have conversations with them.

- Adults will expect you to follow through on whatever you say you'll do.

- Adults will expect you to do your part to help.

- Adults will expect you to make decisions and deal with the consequences.

- Adults will expect that you don't want to be treated like a little kid (and they'll be frustrated if you *act* like a little kid).

Do you see what a major change this is? It's HUGE! Really, it all boils down to two things: responsibility and freedom. You want them both. Adults (parents, teachers, relatives) will start to give them to you, although probably not as quickly, or as much, as you'd like.

We encourage you to enjoy this shift. Show the adults in your life that you can be trusted with responsibility and freedom, and they'll eventually give you more.

8. YOU'RE NOW A MASSIVE MARKETING DEMOGRAPHIC

A *marketing demographic* (yeah, more big words) is just a group of people companies know they can sell stuff to. For example, diaper makers know that while lots of different people buy diapers, most of them are young moms. So they make ads and TV commercials and even diaper packaging with young moms in mind.

Fifty years ago, no one thought young teenagers had any money (because most of them didn't). Companies didn't really exist to sell stuff to teenagers. Maybe a few companies knew they could sell stuff to older teenagers; but none of them was thinking about young teenagers.

But all that has changed. Companies that sell stuff know that young teenagers spend a *ton of money*. And—this is wild—they also know that young teenagers have a major influence on how *their parents* spend money.

As a result, there are thousands and thousands of people whose jobs are to try to figure out how to get you to buy stuff (or to tell your parents that you want them to buy stuff for you). That's why there are so many ads and TV commercials targeted right at you. That's why there are so many stores at the mall that sell stuff *you like*. That's why there are so many Web sites created with *you* in mind.

This was true when you were a little kid also. But it's *way* truer now. And if you start to pay attention to it, then you'll see that you're being sold to all the time. You're constantly hearing messages about stuff you *need*, or stuff that will make your life *better*, or stuff that will make you *more popular*, or stuff that will make you *happier*.

It's really important to learn that the promises of these ads and Web sites and TV commercials are designed only to get you to spend money. They don't really know you. And most of them don't really care if you actually *are* happier or have a better life or anything like that.

Our advice: Get smart about the real purpose of magazine ads, TV commercials, billboards, and all the other gimmicks trying to sell to you. Don't believe all their promises.

9. WHEN AM I GROWN UP?

Now *that's* a great question. (Did we mention we love great questions?) And like lots of *your* questions, the answer isn't simple or easy—or else you probably wouldn't be asking.

Wouldn't it be cool if there were a specific moment you could arrive at "all grown up"? Maybe when you reach five feet tall (and can finally ride all the roller coasters). Or when you get your driver's license. Or how 'bout when you graduate from high school...get your first "real" job...or get married. WHEN is it?

Truth is, we know lots of car-driving, high-school-diploma'd, five-feet-plus people who don't seem very "grown up" at all. In fact, we've seen *each other* behave like pretty immature grown men! (Marko, mostly.)

Being grown up is more of a journey than a destination. When you wake up on your 13th birthday, you can say, "Today, I'm a teenager," but there's no specific day when you can announce, "Today, I'm grown up!"

Think of it like this: You've seen a drooling toddler grab handfuls of food and cram them into her mouth—and all over her lips, chin, cheeks, and hair. Is she eating by herself? Well, sort of. She'll learn to do it better over time. But if she's like us, then there will be moments when she's seven or 12 or 27 and she'll still miss her mouth and spill food all over herself (while her friends crack up). She'll kinda look like a toddler again.

Know this: "Growing up" (a.k.a., *maturity*) is definitely the right goal. Look at what Hebrews 5:12-14 (*The Message*) says about growing up:

BY THIS TIME YOU OUGHT TO BE TEACHERS YOURSELVES,
YET HERE I FIND YOU NEED SOMEONE TO SIT DOWN WITH YOU AND
GO OVER THE BASICS ON GOD AGAIN, STARTING FROM SQUARE ONE—
BABY'S MILK, WHEN YOU SHOULD HAVE BEEN ON SOLID FOOD LONG AGO!
MILK IS FOR BEGINNERS, INEXPERIENCED IN GOD'S WAYS; SOLID FOOD IS
FOR THE MATURE, WHO HAVE SOME PRACTICE IN TELLING RIGHT
FROM WRONG.

Still...cut yourself some slack. You're in middle school—and only partway through the journey. It's okay to still be a kid while you're on the "growing up" adventure.

I WAS A MIDDLE SCHOOL DORK!
—SCOTT

You know the difference between a girlfriend and a friend who's a girl, right?

Well, in seventh grade I hung out with a red-headed girl named Lynn who was *not* my girlfriend, but definitely my friend. (Believe it or not, she ended up marrying my redheaded college roommate, and they now have some redheaded kids. But that's a different story.)

Anyway, guys, you also know how you treat friends of the opposite sex differently than you treat your friends who are dudes. Like, you might kinda tease them, hassle them, and act sorta silly in ways you wouldn't act with another dude. Well, that's how I acted around Lynn.

One thing I liked to do was try to get her in trouble during class. I was an expert at whispering a question to her when the teacher's back was turned. As soon as Lynn started to answer me, the teacher would turn around and catch her talking. Yep—I loved it.

In math class I sat in the desk right in front of Lynn. She was catching on to my strategies by then, so I thought I'd better come up with some new ones. Instead of just turning around and saying something, I figured I'd lean my head straight back—all the way back—and rest it on her desk. What I *didn't* know was that Lynn was holding her sharpened pencil in her fist...with the eraser on the desk...and the lead sticking straight up in the air. I snapped my head back—which drove the pencil straight into the back of my skull. Deep! It made a loud crunching sound (kind of like a knife going into a raw potato), and the pencil stuck there.

I walked to the front of the classroom—with a pencil jutting out of the back of my head— and said to my teacher, "Um...Can I go see the nurse?"

I guess that's the price you pay for harassing a friend who's a girl!

SECTION 2

PHYSICAL DEVELOPMENT

10. WHAT IS PUBERTY?

Does that word—*puberty*—kinda weird you out? We thought it was nothing but weird when we were in middle school. It even *sounds* gross. It always made both of us think about pubic hairs, which totally weirded us out.

So now that we have that out of the way, what is "it"? *Puberty* (ha, we said it again!) is the word used to describe all the changes you're going through—pretty much everything in this book. That's why, in the very first chapter, we joked about naming this book *My Puberty*!

Puberty usually refers to the physical part of the changes you're going through (or will go through). Of course, every human is always going through physical changes. But during puberty, it's like being on super-massive-turbocharged physical change.

Puberty starts when your brain tells it to start. It's a bit hard to understand, really, and even super-smart science dudes and dudettes don't really understand what says "now" for each young teenager. But at some point in time—which is different for every young teenager—the brain says, "Go!" and sends a bunch of hormones racing through your body.

It's really easy to tell when girls start puberty because they have their first period (more about that in chapter 13). And this happens, on average, around 11 years old. But it's totally normal for girls to start puberty a full year (or more) younger than that, or up to a couple of years older than that.

Athletic girls usually have their first period at a slightly older age.

Guys are a couple of years behind the girls. (Just a warning here, guys: You'll feel a bit behind the girls for the next 10 years.) It's not as obvious when, exactly, a guy starts puberty. But if you have a "wet dream" (more about that in chapter 13, too), then that's a pretty good sign you've started puberty. This usually happens anywhere from about 11 to 14 years old, but it can be even later than that and not be a big deal at all.

There you have it. It's not such a weird word after all, is it? Just say it out loud a few times—puberty, Puberty, PUBERTY!

11. SMELLING BAD

Ah, B.O.

I knew the initials for body odor long before I knew what they stood for. Those two little letters meant STINK!

When you're little, sweat's no big deal. But when you get older, somehow the sweat starts to smell. I know this firsthand thanks to the hours I've spent on buses loaded with middle schoolers headed to (and especially *home from*) camp. On this one bus trip, I'm not sure which was worse—the B.O. from the 50 sweaty middle school guys who forgot to take showers all week, or the guy next to me who puked *in my lap*. Both were pretty smelly. Maybe that's why no parents hugged me when I got off the bus...

Do you know what makes sweat *stink*? B.O. is the odor from microscopic bacteria (which everybody has), and these bacteria grow in the presence of sweat. Along with heat, those famous hormones you've heard so much about also kick the stink into higher gear once you hit puberty. (So while Marko may get more warm and sunny days in San Diego than I get here in beautiful Chicago, he gets more chances for B.O., too.)

Like many other things, B.O. "potential" varies from person to person. Some people just sweat more, so they might have to deal with smell issues more. (Note to the guys: This probably means you!) That's life. But if that's *your* situation, here are some simple coping strategies:

- **Don't skip the shower!** It's simply the best way to keep clean—and smelling fresh.

- **Change those clothes, man!** I admit it: I sometimes wear a favorite shirt or pair of jeans for more than one day in a row. But choosing clean clothes each day helps chase the B.O. away.

- **Deodorant is your friend.** Deodorant, antiperspirant, body spray, whichever. It all helps your body fight off the smell factor (along with the shower and clean clothes) so the stink doesn't catch up with ya. (Hey, about those ads that say a certain product will win you dates big time? Well, don't get your hopes up.)

Oh, and don't forget to **brush those teeth**, too. Everyone's mouth is full of bacteria, and there's nothing like morning breath to chase away friends fast—at any time of the day.

"DO I SMELL BAD?"

—TRENT, 7TH GRADE

BODY FACT: EVERY PERSON HAS A UNIQUE TONGUE PRINT (LIKE A FINGERPRINT).

12. AM I NORMAL? WHAT IS NORMAL?

Scott and Marko have worked with thousands of middle schoolers over the years. And here's a fact that might surprise you: We've never ever met young teenagers who, at some point in their young teenage years, didn't think they were developing abnormally (or wrong). Never. Ever.

Let's say that another way: At some point (maybe not always), *all* young teenagers worry that their bodies aren't changing correctly. Maybe you think you're too tall, too short, too heavy, too thin, too lopsided, too funny-sounding, too squeaky, too hairy, not hairy enough, too weak, or even too average. And maybe we didn't cover the word that describes why you believe you're not normal.

Well, here's what *is* normal: Feeling as if you're not normal.

So what's normal physical change? Uh, look in the mirror. Unless you're part of a very, very small percentage of kids who have some issues that a doctor needs to deal with, you are normal.

Here's another thing that's normal: Being a bit "too" something for a while. Because everyone changes at different times, you might get taller than your friends all of a sudden; or they all might get taller than you. You might find your voice changing (especially if you're a guy) when no one else's is; or you might find that lots of other guys' voices are changing, but yours isn't yet. If you're a girl, then you might discover that one of your breasts is bigger than the other one. Don't freak out—that's normal. Oh, and the "hair down there" (pubic hair): Some kids get it early, some get it later.

Think of it as a long-distance race. Some runners start out fast and are a bit slower later on. Some start out slow but gain distance later in the race. By the time you're through your teenage years, you'll be just fine.

13. PERIODS AND WET DREAMS

This is probably one of those chapters you really wanted to read but didn't want anyone to see you reading, right? Yeah, that's normal, too.

Periods (for girls) and wet dreams (for guys) are not the same thing. But they're both things that start to happen near the beginning of puberty (the physical changes you go through in your early teenage years—see chapter 12 for more information). So we're going to talk about both of them in one short chapter.

Let's start with girls and their periods. The female body is an amazing thing, and God did some truly fantastic creative work when he invented women. Women's bodies are *way* more complicated than men's bodies. That's why women have special doctors called "gynecologists" (say GUY-no-college-ist).

A woman's body has a monthly time (the fancy term for it is her *menstrual cycle*, but most people just say "period") when it releases a certain amount of blood. This is all a part of how women are able to have babies. If a woman is pregnant, her body doesn't release that blood because she needs it for the baby. But when she's not pregnant, she has a monthly period. It's not dirty or gross—it's just a normal part of life. Sometimes a period can make a woman (or a teenage girl) feel kind of moody or even have some physical pain. That's also normal.

Girls, it's really important that you talk to your mom about this subject. And if you don't live with a mom, then you need to find another adult woman to talk to.

Now, for the guys. Once you start puberty, your testicles start producing semen (a fluid—not urine) that carries sperm. Sperm is the stuff that makes it possible for you to become a dad someday. Semen builds up a little bit at a time. And when it's not needed for sex, it has to be released some other way. This almost always happens during a "wet dream." (The fancy term is *nocturnal emission*—*nocturnal* means "at night" and *emission* means "something that comes out of you.") You'll find, if you haven't already, that you'll start to wake up once in a while with a white sticky fluid in your underwear or on your bed sheets. Listen: You shouldn't feel embarrassed about this. It's completely normal. It even happens to grown men.

Remember, periods and wet dreams are part of God's design for you. They're a part of you becoming an adult.

14. GROWTH PAIN

There's a strange pain many teenagers experience that will never happen again during their lives: Growth pain. Most teenagers will go through what people call a "growth spurt" a few times. This just means that you start getting taller at a pretty quick rate.

You've probably seen this: Some kid in your class was short before summer break but came back in the fall—well, less short.

Or maybe you've experienced a time in the last year or two when you hadn't seen some relatives or friends of the family for a year or so (like grand-parents who live far away), and when they see you they exclaim, "Wow! You've grown like a weed!"

Because girls usually start puberty earlier than boys, they often get taller than boys (or taller than *some* boys) for a couple of years. And girls, on av-erage, reach their full adult height by their mid-teens, while most guys don't reach their full adult height until much later in their teenage years (and sometimes into their early twenties). This height difference can be awkward for shorter boys and for taller girls.

When you *do* go through one of those periods when you're growing in height at a quick rate, you'll sometimes experience pain in your legs. It feels like it's deep inside—like it's in your bones. You'll often feel it at night when you're lying in bed trying to get to sleep. And it'll even keep you awake because the pain is distracting.

There's not a whole lot that can be done about this (other than asking your mom or dad for some aspirin). Sorry. We wish we had a simple "snap your fingers three times and the pain will go away" solution for you.

But remember this: Massive change of any sort (in people, in companies, in countries) is always messy—even when it's a good change. And massive change of any sort also usually includes some pain—even when the change is good. So when you're lying in your bed, trying to get to sleep, and feeling frustrated with the growth pain in your legs, remember that you're morphing into an adult. Oh, and don't forget to ask for an aspirin.

"WHY AM I TALLER THAN EVERYONE ELSE?"

—SANDRA, 6TH GRADE

15. BODY SHAPE

Besides getting taller, there's another major change that happens to your body during your teenage years. It's the shape of your body.

Little kids' body shapes are pretty simple, right? Sure, some are rounder than others, and some are thinner than others. But other than that, the body shapes of children don't vary much from one to the next. However, women and men have all kinds of variety in their shapes.

Women have differing breast sizes, hip sizes, waist sizes, and many other things (like neck length, leg length, shoulder sizes, and more). The same is true for men, with some of the main differences being in their chest size, leg and arm size and length, and neck size. If you look at a bunch of adults, then you'll see a wide variety of body shapes.

These changes will start happening while you're in your young teenage years (especially for girls; some guys don't start to see this change until their middle teenage years). And sometimes the in-between shapes are a bit awkward.

We're sure you've seen someone blow up a balloon animal before. Well, when the air is going into the balloon—when it's in the midst of changing from a limp piece of stretchy plastic to an inflated wiener dog or whatever—there are moments when the shape is, well, less than perfect. Maybe the balloon-dog's body is nicely plump with air, but the head and the legs are still lifeless and wimpy.

Eventually, after all the blowing up and bending and twisting and tying, everything seems to even out.

That's a good way of thinking about how your body is going to change during your teenage years. Guys often find that their feet grow really big before the rest of their body catches up. Both guys and girls can find themselves either putting on a bunch of weight or suddenly slimming down. Legs. Arms. Neck. Feet. Waistline. Chest. Rear end. You name it—it's changing.

Don't freak about your body shape. Like the balloon animal (that's kind of a lame example, isn't it?), you'll turn out just fine in the end.

16. ZITS

It's happened millions of times to millions of people.

You wake up, stumble to the mirror, focus your eyes...and there it is—a giant zit. Acne. A pimple. Maybe a whole herd of 'em are scattered across your face.

We remember the feelings that come with zits— *UGH! How can I hide this thing? Why me? Why now?* (And they always show up at the worst times. I remember when I got a zit the size of Detroit right between my eyes the same week a girl I liked asked me to a school dance. AARGH!)

THE SOURCE

A zit is simply a blocked pore in your skin. Everybody's skin has some natural oil in it. But when a pore gets blocked, the oil piles up and creates that irritating whitehead, blackhead, or frustrating red pimple—they all begin in a similar way.

NOT THE SOURCE

You didn't do anything to cause the zits. They're a cruddy part of puberty for most people. Some say bad eating creates zits, but there's no evidence that junk food, sugar, or anything else makes zits worse. (So eat your Skittles without guilt.) Acne isn't caused by not washing enough, either. Remember, the oil's coming from *inside* your skin—not outside. (Even so, check out chapter 11 for a quick review.)

WHAT MAKES IT WORSE?

Try to avoid 1) digging at your zits, 2) real intense sunlight, and 3) oily stuff (lotions and makeup). But the biggest irritator can actually be *stress*. Fighting off stress isn't simple sometimes, but it can be done. Talk to someone you trust about it.

ONE MORE *CRUCIAL* THING

Check out what God says to Samuel in 1 Samuel 16:7—"Do not consider his appearance or his height, for I have rejected him. The LORD does not look at the things human beings look at. People look at the outward appearance, but the LORD looks at the heart." Even when your *outside* (skin, hair, body, whatever) doesn't look how you want it to, you *really are* incredibly valuable—beyond what you can even imagine. Sure, your appearance can affect the way you feel. But don't let it affect what you *believe* about yourself. Even when things are crazy-hard, God's SO not limited by a few zits. He's still working IN YOU.

P.S. You'll ultimately outgrow most acne. But I actually got a zit in that same spot between my eyes the week I wrote this. Come on!

"I LOVE TO POP THEM!"

—CHRIS, 7TH GRADE

17. THE IMPORTANCE OF SLEEP

Okay, we (Marko and Scott) want to be the cool youth worker guys. And we know that talking about your getting enough sleep is *not* the guaranteed way to be the cool youth worker guys. So we *could* say, "Hey, let's stay up all night long and party! Woo hoo!"

But, uh, then there's this little thing we'd have to deal with called guilt. Why would we feel guilty? Because we've learned something really surprising recently: Brain doctors only figured this out in the past 10 years or so (which is why we just learned it). Here it is: Your brain isn't done growing. There are two main parts of your brain that continue to grow and form throughout your teenage years (and into your early 20s). And they're both really important parts.

The first part of your brain that's not done growing is the one right behind your forehead. If you want to impress your science teacher, then you can say it's the "prefrontal cortex"; it's the part of your brain that helps you make good decisions. The other parts of your brain that aren't done growing yet are on both sides of your head—behind your temples. This is why they're called the "temporal lobes." These bad boys help you understand emotions—especially other people's.

But here's what's really crazy: The main way to help those parts of your brain grow in a healthy way is by sleeping. Yup, sleep. You'd think the best way to grow your brain would be to think really hard, but those parts grow best with lots and lots of sleep. To say it another way, they can be hurt by *not* getting enough sleep.

How much sleep do you think you need? Six hours? Eight hours? Nope. Actually 10 full hours. If you don't get 10 full hours of sleep on a regular basis, then you're actually making it difficult for your brain to grow the way it's supposed to.

So that's why we (Marko and Scott) would feel guilty if we told you to stay up all night long. We'd be telling you to hurt your brain.

"HOW DO YOU GET ANY SLEEP WHEN YOU HAVE SO MUCH HOMEWORK AND YOU JUST HAD SOCCER PRACTICE?"

—MELISSA, 7TH GRADE

18. EATING DISORDERS

Our bodies need food, right? And different factors (like when we last ate or whether we like what's for dinner) influence what, when, and how much we eat.

Have you ever heard of an eating disorder? It messes up a person's eating in ways that are both physically and emotionally damaging. It could be eating way too much (using food to try to feel better when things are rough), eating way too little (trying to get the "perfect body"), or eating a lot and then making yourself throw up so you don't gain weight (which is *way* unsafe).

Eating disorders are complicated. Part of the problem happens when the world around us puts too much importance on having a "perfect" appearance. Think about it: Magazine models, TV stars, rock singers—we get an image of what "perfect" should be like from celebrities whose flaws have been airbrushed away. And it messes with us. When I (Scott) was in middle school, I was reeeeeally skinny. I had buddies who looked like they'd jumped off the pages of a muscle magazine. And honestly, it bugged me. I wondered why I didn't get the body that turned the girls' heads.

It's not wrong to want to look good or to be in shape. (Actually, some of us need to fall off the couch and get some exercise.) But if your wish to look "perfect" becomes almost all you can think about, that's dangerous...very dangerous.

If your thoughts are dominated by what you see (or what you *think* you see) when you look in the mirror, please—**talk to someone!** This is the biggest, MOST important step to take. If you're starving yourself, stuffing yourself, throwing up, or using food in a way that has nothing to do with your hunger, then get help. It's going to take a caring adult to help you tackle this issue. And don't start thinking you're bad or at fault for struggling in this area—that's not true. It's good to get help—and you're worth it.

When you do look in the mirror, look deeper than your body. God put a valuable soul inside you—one that God absolutely treasures. The body you're walking around in is just the "wrapper" for your soul. Who you are on the *inside* really does matter most, even when our culture tells you differently.

19. COMPARISON

You know what it means to compare things, right? You notice the ways they're the same or the ways they're different. People do this *all the time*, and there's a good chance you'll always find yourself comparing something of yours with something that belongs to someone else.

Their house is larger. Her car is nicer. His bike is way sweeter than mine. Her purse was way more expensive than mine.

The comparisons don't stop with stuff—they're often made between bodies, too. *Her hair is longer. He's way more buff than me. She's so naturally thin.*

This kind of comparison really kicks into high gear during your young teenage years, and for a few understandable reasons:

- You're changing so much, you really notice yourself (and your body) more than you did a couple of years ago.

- Your brain is working in new ways that it didn't a few years ago, and it's better at making comparisons.

- The world around you—the ads you see, the TV you watch—all of it is *trying* to get you to compare yourself with others your age.

Try on this idea for a minute: Spending your time and effort on making comparisons, especially when it comes to your body, is both a silly waste of time and a bit of an insult to God.

See, it's a silly waste of time because comparing your body to someone else's doesn't change your body. The only thing it does is convince you that something's wrong with you (which isn't true—see chapter 12).

But spending a bunch of time comparing your body with others' is also an insult to God. Yup. It's kind of like saying, "God, you were clueless when you made me, and you really messed up!" Well, if you *do* feel like saying that to God, then it's not like God will zap you with zits or something. God loves you. And God is okay with your not understanding everything, including his reasons. But still, God created you. God is stoked about you. God is totally into you.

Our suggestion: Find contentment in who you are and know that your body is going to continue changing, massively, in the next few years.

SECTION 3

MY BRAIN AND
MY THOUGHTS

20. BRAIN DEVELOPMENT

Do you ever think about that mushy lump of grey stuff behind your face? (Uh, we mean your brain, not that chunk o' somethin' you found up your nose.) Your brain is, in our opinion, one of God's most amazing inventions. It's a living computer, more powerful than anything ever made. Scientists are learning stuff about the brain all the time, but we still only partly understand it.

This might surprise you: Your brain is still growing. We don't just mean that your skull, along with the rest of your body, is growing and your brain is getting a bit larger. We mean there are new parts of your brain that are still developing. Isn't that wild?

It'd be like if you'd been riding this one bike for a couple of years, and then the bike suddenly started to "grow" a new part—a part that would make the bike work WAY better, go faster, be more stable.

Here are two brain-bit highlights that you'll grow into during the next few years:

1. BRAIN HIGHWAY

First, there are these microscopic connections all over your brain—millions of 'em—called "neurons" (say NUR-ons). They're like the roads that connect all the information; they're the connections that make your brain work, make it possible for you to think. During your teenage years, these neurons grow an outer coating, kind of like putting on a wetsuit. But—are you ready for this?—this new coating makes information travel up to 200 percent faster along your neurons. Dude! That means you're ready for some big-time brain stuff.

2. GIANT FOREHEAD
Then there's this part of your brain that's just now starting to really grow. It's the part right behind your forehead. It's not like there's a big empty space there now. It's more like the structure is there, but it's not wired yet. That part of your brain is really important. It's the decision-making center of the brain, and it helps you think about possibilities (like thinking through your different options before making a decision). It's also the part of the brain that helps you think about consequences.

You gotta protect your noggin. There are some really cool changes going on up there that will help you for the rest of your life. (We were just kidding about the giant forehead, by the way.)

21. WHY ALL THE *AHA'S*? WHY DOES EVERYTHING SEEM SO COMPLICATED?

BODY FACT: IF ALL THE BLOOD VESSELS IN YOUR BODY WERE LAID END TO END, THEY WOULD REACH ABOUT 60,000 MILES. (AND WHEN YOU'RE AN ADULT, THEY'LL SPAN 100,000 MILES!)

Have you ever thought to yourself, *Why does everything seem so complicated now? When I was younger, things seemed really simple.*

That's a super-normal thing to think. And most of the answer has to do with your brain. (Some of it also has to do with the fact that, as a young teenager, you're experiencing more of the world than you were as, say, a nine-year-old.)

We've said this a ton already, but we're gonna say it again: You're going through a massive time of change. Your brain is also changing in huge ways. Some of the changes in your brain are making it so you can understand stuff you've never understood before. That's why it seems like you have a lot of *aha's.* You know what we mean by that, right? Like, when you suddenly understand something or suddenly have an insight you've never had before? That's because your growing and changing brain is making all kinds of new thinking possible.

It's as if your brain were a house. Right now you're finding a bunch of new doors and windows and hallways and rooms you didn't know were there before. Cool, huh?

But (yeah, you knew there was going to be a "but," didn't you?) there's the other side to all of this. Now that your brain is growing and changing like crazy, and now that you can think in new kinds of ways, and now that you can understand things in new ways—things are more confusing.

Think of it this way: Let's say you're playing with Legos. You have 100 Lego pieces, so your options are pretty limited. You've played with the same 100 Lego pieces for a few years now, and you've built about everything you can imagine. It's simple (that's like being a 10-year-old). Then for a few years you get new Lego pieces every day—sometimes dozens of them. This creates all kinds of new building possibilities (like the *aha's* we just talked about). But it also makes the whole building process more complicated, especially when you have one thousand or even ten thousand Lego pieces. Does that make sense?

Okay, now go build a brain with your old Legos. (We're kidding.)

22. ABSTRACT THINKING

This one might be a little hard to understand. So tighten your seatbelt, and read slowly.

As you grow up, your brain goes through a bunch of different stages in how it understands stuff. The last stage is one you start growing into when you begin puberty, but it takes a bunch of years to really get it.

This new ability is called "abstract thinking," and it basically means you develop the ability to think about thinking. Weird, huh? If you're 11 or 12, then you have only a little bit of this ability. But if you're 13 or 14, then you have a little bit more. You won't really know how to use your abstract thinking ability until you're in your older teenage years.

What's it mean? Well, it means you can now (you couldn't as a little kid) think about possibilities, about what *might* be or *might* happen. It means you can think about what life would be like if you were someone else. And more stuff like that.

But this new thinking ability is also kinda like a brand-new muscle. (It's not really a muscle—but pretend with us.) You've never used this muscle, so it's wimpy and weak. It takes years of using your abstract thinking to help it get stronger.

This will have a lot of impact on your life during the next few years. It means you can experience emotions in all new ways. It means you'll start to think about who you really are and who you want to be. And it also means you'll start thinking about spiritual stuff differently (God stuff, that is). In fact, you've probably started doing this already. And that's cool because you want to have a faith that will make sense as you grow up, not one that holds on to the beliefs of a little kid.

Wanna grow your ability to think abstractly? Start thinking about thinking. Try thinking about things that are confusing to you. Try thinking about what you really believe, and why you believe those things.

23. LEFT BRAIN/RIGHT BRAIN

Your brain is such an amazing thing. God really did some of his best work on that three-pound ball o' mush.

Here's something you may have heard at school sometime. Your brain has two halves (usually called—duh—"the left brain" and "the right brain." It probably took hundreds of brilliant scientists to come up with those names, huh?) The two halves are completely separate, except for a ropelike connection thing between them. It's almost like you have two supercomputers joined by a high-speed connection.

Except, get this: Neither half of your brain could work well all on its own. The two halves need each other, but they also have different roles.

The left brain is the part that works best thinking about things like math and science, organization, details, and stuff like that. It's usually a bit stronger than the other half of the brain (kinda like the smart but bossy older brother). And remember, it can't really do what it does without the help of the right side.

The right brain is the part that does best with creativity, music, art, dreaming, and other stuff like that.

Most people are stronger on one side or the other (people call them "left-brain thinkers" or "right-brain thinkers"). And that often plays a role in what kind of job a person gets, what their hobbies are, and what they're skilled in doing. But the people who really change the world are usually strong on both sides of their brain.

So here's our suggestion (brain dudes that we are): If you think you're a super-organized, math-and-science-lovin', left-brain thinker, spend some time doing creative stuff to strengthen your right brain. And if you're a creative, music-loving, artsy type, then try to spend some time doing left-brain stuff to make it stronger.

Remember: Two brains are better than one.

24. ARE ALL GUYS GOOD AT MATH AND SCIENCE? ARE ALL GIRLS GOOD AT ENGLISH AND SOCIAL STUDIES?

Have you ever heard that guys are better at math and science and girls are better at reading, writing, history, and other stuff like that? Whether or not you've heard it, it's something most people believe (ask your parents and see what they say).

So is it true? Yes. And no.

Here's the *yes* part: In the past, most tests have shown this to be true—that guys do better in math and science, and girls do better in reading and writing.

Here's the *no* part: Most people who study this kind of stuff believe it has less to do with any differences between a guy's brain and a girl's brain and more to do with how schools have taught these subjects and what culture has said boys should do and girls should do. For instance, 100 years ago it was difficult to find a top female scientist. But it was also almost impossible for women to succeed in scientific fields because lots of universities didn't allow women to attend, and most people didn't believe women should have careers like that.

This has changed a lot in the last 30 years. And, now there are lots of women who are super-successful in areas that were normally thought to be "male careers." And vice versa—with guys doing well in areas that had been viewed as "female." (Like, nurses were almost always women a long time ago, but nursing schools are full of young men these days.)

Here's the bottom line, and we really hope you'll believe us (even though we might sound a little bit like your parents): You can do well in any academic subject, and it doesn't have anything to do with you being female or male. Of course, some people (of both genders) will be better than others at doing some stuff. But if you're a girl who loves math and science, then don't even think for a second that you shouldn't be "into it" because you're a girl. And the same goes for guys who do well in English, literature (books), writing, and stuff like that.

Don't listen to anyone who tells you what you can't do or who you can't be.

25. DIFFERENT LEARNING STYLES

A personal story from Marko: My daughter, Liesl, had a hard time in middle school because she's super-creative, but the school she was attending didn't have much room for super-creative kids. They wanted her to learn in a way that wasn't creative and that didn't work for her. So after she had a really hard year in sixth grade, we moved Liesl to a different school that uses tons of creative ways to teach. And she's doing fantastic. She loves school, and she's a great student.

The reason for this kind of story is that we all have different ways we learn best. For some people, reading a book is the best way to learn. For others, called "auditory learners," listening to something is best. For still others, called "tactile learners," they learn best when they're using their hands, when they're making something.

Think about how you learn best. Do you doodle and draw little pictures the whole time you're listening to a teacher? Does that actually *help* you learn better? That says something about your learning style.

Or maybe you learn best when you're building something or painting something or writing something (instead of listening or reading). Those things all say something about your learning style.

You might not have the chance to change schools, like Marko's daughter did. But it's helpful to be aware of the way you learn best so you can start to take classes (when you have a chance to choose them yourself) that will allow for that. And even when you have to take a class that uses a learning style that doesn't fit perfectly with yours, you can try to make your learning style a part of how you do your work.

Here's a good thing to think about: God made you wonderfully unique. There's no one exactly like you. Your unique learning style is a part of that. And that part of you is totally cool!

26. SPECULATION

We talked about this a little bit in chapter 22: "Abstract Thinking." But we thought it would be good to talk about it a little more because it's such a big deal.

Here's a question for you. Try to answer honestly (no one will know but you). Do you want your brain to get smarter? Most middle schoolers we know would answer yes to that. Really, most people of *any* age would answer yes to that!

Well, if you want your middle school brain to grow smarter (yes, this really is possible), then you need to learn a big word and practice doing it. Here's the big word, ready? (You can impress your parents and teachers with this one.) *Speculation* (say speck-you-LAY-shun). It's the title of this chapter, so you're probably not too surprised.

Speculation means to think about what *might be*. Let's say you and your friends build a bike ramp. No one has tried it, and somehow you're up first. All your friends are watching, and you're sitting on your bike in front of a house down the street, just thinking about jumping. You ask yourself a specu-lation question: *If I do this, what might happen?* Then you start to speculate about the possibilities. You might sail through the air to the cheers of your friends, post a video on YouTube, and become a national hero. You might jump about two feet and look like a dork. Or you might crash into the ramp—even worse, crash on the other side of the ramp—

and look like an even bigger dork. All that thinking is just speculation because you don't know for sure what's really going to happen.

That kind of thinking—speculation—is brand new to you. Little kids can't really think that way (their brains don't work like that yet). But you can. And if you speculate a lot, it actually helps your brain get smarter. Cool, huh?

Get in the habit of speculating. When you hear your youth group leader talking about something from the Bible, ask yourself, *What would it look like for me to really put this into practice in my life?* When your teacher is talking about some new thing (in any subject), ask yourself, *What would it look like if everyone in the world started doing this thing or believing this thing?*

Woo hoo! Let's hear it for brains that are getting smarter—yours, that is!

27. THE GOOD AND BAD OF DAYDREAMING

Marko's sister had a best friend in middle school who liked to daydream all the time. She rarely paid attention to the teacher, and she was usually staring off into space, dreaming about something. One day in science class, the teacher asked Teresa to go over to a table at the side of the room and take the top off a jar that contained an experiment. But Teresa didn't hear the teacher because she was daydreaming. The teacher asked her again, and Teresa still didn't hear the instructions. Now the teacher was angry and yelled, "Teresa!" This she heard, and she sat up straight in her desk. The teacher continued, "I said, take the top off!" Teresa was totally confused and a little bit scared. So without thinking, she started to take her own top off.

Not a good middle school moment for Teresa. She heard about that story from her friends and classmates all through middle school—and high school.

You know what daydreaming is, right? It's when you're not noticing anything around you, and you're just creating a story in your mind. It's a cool thing. Really, it's a gift from God—the ability to dream about things that might be or even dream about things that will never be.

But daydreaming can also have a bad side, and not only if you do something embarrassing (like Teresa did). For some people, daydreaming becomes a way of running away from the real world.

They escape to their minds and dream up stories of the life they'd like to have. If you do this all the time, then you'll never actually deal with the real world.

Another way that daydreaming (and creating fantasies) can be not so good is when you start to want the life you dream up—even when it's not possible. Marko used to spend a lot of time—in middle school, and for years afterward—dreaming about what it would be like to be really, really rich. He'd create entire stories in his mind of what he'd do with the money. Over and over again he'd revisit these stories.

Here's what's difficult about this: Some of it is good, but too much of it can be bad. And we can't give you a perfect description of where to draw that line. Here's a thought, though: If most of your daydreaming is about you getting stuff, or about you becoming popular, or about you getting revenge on the people who are mean to you, then it's not a good thing. See, those aren't the things God really wants for you in life anyhow.

But if you want to spend a bunch of time daydreaming about things that would please God—making the world a better place, showing love to others, becoming who God made you to be—then GO FOR IT! Daydream away!

I WAS A MIDDLE SCHOOL DORK!
—MARKO

Omigosh. I can hardly believe I did this.

It's barely even a funny story. It's really just a story that shows how completely lame and idiotic I was (like, um, many middle school boys).

I had an acoustic guitar. I didn't know how to play it, and it wasn't nice or valuable. So my friends Chris and Chris (really) and I decided to smash it to pieces. Not only that, but we also took pictures of ourselves smashing it while we (and this is the part that made it ultimately cool in our minds, and ultimately stupid in my parents' minds) jumped off the garage roof.

Yes, this is true. I'm not quite sure how we decided it was safe to jump off the garage roof. But we figured out how to climb up there from the top of a fence. And somehow we figured out how to land into a roll—a somersault—so we didn't smash our ankles or break any bones when we hit the ground.

So we took turns jumping with the guitar and smashing it as we went. And we took pictures of the whole thing—lots of them. We—me and the Chrisses—thought it was the funniest thing ever. My parents strongly disagreed with us on that one. They did *not* find it funny, not even a little bit.

I'm 44 years old now. Recently, I was looking through some old photo albums, and I found those guitar-smashing-roof-jumping photos. Here's the super-dork part: I still think it's funny.

SECTION 4

IDENTITY

28. WHAT IS IDENTITY?

If we're going to have a whole section about identity, then we think it'd be a good idea to start with this question: What *is* identity?

Identity, to make it short and sweet, is your understanding of who you are. It's not what you can do, or what you look like, or even who someone else says you are. It's who you really are; and, more specifically, it's who you understand yourself to be.

The term *ID* is short for "identification." Your parents probably have driver's licenses, which are considered ID. You might carry a school ID or some other kind of ID card. That little card says stuff about you—stuff that is uniquely you. It usually includes a picture of you, as well as some other information.

But whatever information is listed on that ID isn't your real identity.

We (Marko and Scott) remember when we were middle schoolers; we were just starting to think about who we were, what made us unique, how we were different from and the same as our parents, how we were different from and the same as our best friends. Those thoughts are the beginning work of figuring out your identity.

Today, we could say all these things about ourselves:

- I'm a dad

- I'm a son

- I'm a husband

- I'm a follower of Jesus

- I'm a youth worker

- I'm an author (Hey, you're reading a book we wrote!)

- I'm a movie lover

But that's just a start. What *kind* of dad am I, and what *kind* of dad do I want to be? Because there are lots of different ways to be a dad, right?

One of the reasons our culture started making space for the teenage years (remember, the teenage years weren't even recognized in our culture as an age group until a little more than 100 years ago) was to allow people your age to figure out their identities. It's a long and challenging process. And you'll probably think of yourself in lots of different ways over the next several years—that's okay.

Ask yourself: Who am I, really? Who do I want to become? And, most importantly, who did God make me to be?

"I'M CHANGING SO MUCH. I FEEL SO CONFUSED ON WHO I REALLY AM."
—MALINDA, 8TH GRADE

29. WHY IS MY IDENTITY IMPORTANT NOW?

Why did our culture start to make space (the teenage years) for students to figure out their identities? Well, it's all about maturity. Your brain couldn't handle thinking about stuff like this until now. And once you *do* get it somewhat figured out, you'll be better prepared to be an adult.

An adult who doesn't know who he is (who doesn't have his identity figured out, at least somewhat) will always struggle with everything he does in life. He'll struggle with his job (because he won't be sure it's the right job for who he is). He'll struggle with his commitments (because he's not sure if he's committed to the right things). He'll struggle with his marriage and other important relationships (because all relationships are built on understanding yourself and the other person you're in a relationship with).

From the time you start puberty—or about the time you start middle school—to, normally, somewhere in your early 20s (the next 10 years or so), you'll be wrestling with this identity issue. It might seem totally unimportant or confusing to you right now, and that's totally fine. Much of this struggle will happen naturally, without you really trying. But it's great to start thinking about it.

Don't try to figure it all out right now. You'll discover new things about yourself in the next few years that will become important parts of your identity. And you'll probably *think* you've got it

78

figured out a few times along the way, only to discover you were a bit off—or even way off.

30. TRYING EVERYTHING

We wonder if you've noticed this, as we have: Older teenage athletes often focus on one sport, while younger teenagers typically play more than one sport.

Or maybe you've noticed that you keep finding new things you'd like to try. In fact, have you ever had a parent or teacher or another adult say to you, in frustration, "Why don't you just stick with one thing? Finish something!"

This week water polo sounds really fun—and playing the drums. Next week you might think you'd like to try art classes. But only for a couple of days because then you're thinking it would be cool to go to some auditions and do some acting.

If it sounds like we've been watching your life (even if the specifics are a little different), it's be-cause...we've installed cameras in your room and your house and all over your school and everywhere you go. Bwa-ha-ha-ha (evil laughter)!

No, not really. That would create all kinds of problems.

Really, we know you're probably like this be-cause, well, all middle school students—or at least most of them—are like this. You try something new this month, and then you think about trying some-thing different the next month.

Can you guess what we're going to say? (We've said it more than once in this nifty little book.) IT'S OKAY! You're normal. In fact, it's *important* that you try lots of new stuff. It's all part of figuring out your identity—figuring out what you're good at doing, what you like to do, and what makes you unique.

So don't apologize for trying new stuff—although finishing things can be good, too.

31. "IDENTITY SHOPPING"

Hey, if you haven't read the last chapter (about trying new things), go read it first. It's kind of like Part One of a two-parter.

Okay. We're good to go?

There's another part of "trying new things" that goes quite a bit further than just trying new things. And it can cause some problems. We're calling it "identity shopping." It's when you don't just try new things, but you try being a whole different person.

Here's what we mean. When you're into something, you often hang with other kids who are also into that thing. If you play soccer, then you spend time with the team. If you're in band, then you spend time with other band kids. You might attend a church youth group, so of course you spend time with the youth group kids. You might also have friends who don't fit into any of those other groups, but you hang with them on weekends.

Most of these groups have things that hold them together (more than just "we're on a soccer team" or "we're in band"). There are usually jokes and slang and even things like music choices and clothes that each group considers okay. The result? *When you go from one group to another, you may feel like you have to become a different person.*

Here's the tricky part: *Some* of this is normal and a part of starting to figure out that identity thing. But *too much* of it becomes a problem. If you get really good at being a different person when you're in different situations, then you won't know how to shut that off when you grow older, and you'll end up creating all kinds of problems for yourself.

In the long run—trust us on this—you'll be happier if you're just *one* person, not trying to be a whole bunch of different people in different settings.

32. WHAT SHAPES MY IDENTITY?

When I (Marko) was in seventh grade, the youth pastor at my church stopped me in the hallway between services. There were tons of people around, all noisy and bumping into each other, and the youth pastor looked at me and said, "Hey, Oestreicher," (that's my last name—don't bother trying to pronounce it). He continued, "You'd be a really good youth pastor some day."

Whoa! I never forgot that one little sentence. I did become a youth pastor, and I've worked with teenagers ever since—for about 25 years now!

So, did that youth pastor *make* me a youth pastor? No. I chose to become one. But lots of other people and things also shaped me.

See, your identity—who you really are—is shaped by many things, not just your choices. A kid who grows up in a home with artsy parents who take him to the art museum every weekend, talk about art, get private art lessons for him, and have a painting studio in their house will be—duh! obvious!—much more likely to end up as an artist than, say, a kid who grows up with parents who hate art.

But the influences on your identity are more than just what your parents do or what they're like (although those things can be a huge influence). Your identity—as you start to figure it out over the next several years—will be shaped by experiences in life, people you meet, music and movies and TV and books and magazines, teachers, friends, and lots more. Whew! That's a big list of influences. Makes us tired just thinking about it.

It's good to realize that all these forces are influencing you. But here's the super-mega-massive-mondo-ultra-humongous piece of advice we have for you (really, this is worth the price of the book right here): **You have to *choose* what things and what people you want to influence your identity, to influence who you are. If you don't choose, then *everything* will influence you. And that's a very confusing way to live.**

33. DO I REALLY HAVE A CHOICE? OR IS IT FATE?

When I (Scott) was a little kid, I did some dumb things—like the time I flushed my sister's Barbie doll down the toilet. But I remembered hearing in church that "God knows everything about us"—what we've done and even what we're *going* to do. So when I got busted for clogging the plumbing with that soaking-wet Barbie—I pointed the finger straight at God. Pretty cool, I thought. It made *sense* to blame God. After all, God knew I was going to do it, so it was kinda actually God's fault, right?

Yeah, not so much. It sure didn't get me off the hook.

Why? Because the truth is that *choosing* is one of the coolest gifts God's given to us.

Joshua 24:15 says, "But if serving the LORD seems undesirable to you, then choose for yourselves this day whom you will serve...But as for me and my household, we will serve the LORD."

Like we talked about in the last chapter, it's true that there are some factors you can't control. But there are tons that you CAN! Think of all the decisions you make every day:

- Shoes or sandals

- Jeans or shorts

- Dr. Pepper or Mountain Dew

- MTV or ESPN

- Talk or be quiet

- Skatepark, video games, or homework

- iPod or iMovie

- Break a rule or obey it

It's been said that Your Life = The Sum of All Your Decisions.

When you're in middle school, it's easy to think about all the stuff that gets decided for you: What town you live in...what teacher you have...what your body looks like. You can see lots of things you CAN'T control—and you'd be right. But what you CAN control—what you get to decide—is how you *choose* to react to that stuff.

If you're willing to change your view and see the gazillion choices you DO have—then you might realize that God gave you more control than you first thought.

But guess what? That's YOUR choice.

34. IT'S OKAY NOT TO HAVE IT ALL FIGURED OUT

Who am I, really?

What am I going to be?

Where does God want me to end up?

Why are things so *hard* sometimes?

Sometimes you might feel the pressure of questions like those. Maybe BIG pressure. Here's what we want to tell you:

IT'S OKAY...it's even normal!

When you look around a room full of people, you can make lots of observations. But you CAN'T see what's on their minds. So, interestingly, it often looks as if other people aren't wrestling with some of the same questions you are. It might seem as if they've got things *figured out*, which can make you feel as if YOU also should have things *figured out*.

We'll let you in on a little secret:

NOBODY's got it all *figured out*!

Doubts, worries, uncertainties, trouble—they're all going to come your way. In fact, Jesus promised it. Yep—*promised* it. Some people think that by following Jesus, all of that uncomfortable stuff will go away and a perfect life will start. But Jesus never said that. In John 16:33 he said, "In this world you will have trouble" (emphasis mine). Not "you *might*" or "*some* of you will." Everybody! And it won't always be easy to figure out. But the verse continues (and I love this part), "But take heart! I have overcome the world."

God doesn't say you're going to get everything solved…figured out…or even mostly explained. But what God *does* promise is that he's not going to leave you alone in it. Over and over in the Bible, God promises to be *with* you.

So what does that mean? Well, God wants to hear your thoughts and concerns. God wants to whisper his thoughts to you and remind you that you're not alone. God often uses other people to help with that. So get real with a parent, relative, or friend so they can listen to you. It takes guts to share your questions, and there are no guarantees on getting things "solved." But being *alone* with your problem stinks—so share it with someone.

And you might be surprised to find out just how "normal" you are.

35. INTERESTS

BODY FACT: THE LONGEST FINGERNAILS MEASURED 24 FEET 7 INCHES IN LENGTH.

What are you into?

Your interests can say a lot about you. Or not! I'm (Scott) into playing darts, reading, and messing with computers. But that doesn't mean I'm a geek...I'm pretty sure.

Instead of worrying about what anyone else thinks about your interests, middle school's an amaaazing time to dig further into discovering what you're into.

OLD INTERESTS

Now that you're a little older, try pushing your interests to the next level. Take what you already like—whether it's skateboards, cheerleading, drawing, computers, video cameras, biking, horses, soccer, inventing, reading, ostrich racing, booger flicking (oops, got carried away there)—and think about how you can look at it from a *new angle*.

Instead of just riding skateboards and bikes, what about getting a job at a local bike shop or even volunteering there for a few hours? The people there are already interested in the same stuff you are—and you can learn more about it from them.

Or instead of just watching videos, what if you looked into *making* your own videos or learning techniques to make them better? You're more capable than you were just a short time ago—so dive deeper into the areas that already grab your attention. Old-interests-with-a-new-twist could be a blast!

NEW INTERESTS

This time of your life is also perfect for *checking out new stuff.* What's something you've always wanted to try, but you just haven't done it yet? C'mon, dream a little! Maybe you've got a friend who's been into a sport, activity, or hobby that you've always thought was cool and maybe worth trying. Why not try it now? We know tons of people who've done that and ended up being better at it than the friends who got them involved in the first place.

ONE-TIME CHALLENGE

Ever been afraid to try something even though you kind of wanted to? We have, too! What about taking the "one-time" approach? Tell yourself, *I'm going to give this a shot and see how it goes.* The thrill of trying something—with no pressure to be any good at it—is exciting. And if you end up being no good at it—who cares? If you don't try, you'll never know.

BUT what if you happened to end up being *great* at it? Now THAT could be interesting!

36. TAKING RESPONSIBILITY/ BLAMING OTHERS

This is a BIG one. Learning to take responsibility for what you do (and not just pointing the finger at someone else when things go wrong) is a *sure* sign of maturity. Unfortunately, it's a lesson many adults haven't even mastered yet.

Little kids have a two-word phrase they love to say whenever they get asked a tough question. Remember it? *Not me!*

"Who ate a red Popsicle on the couch and left half of it between the cushions?"

Not me!

"Who forgot to turn off the water in the bathtub, so there's now a waterfall flowing over the edge of the tub and a river running out the door and down the hall?"

Not me!

"Who stepped in mud and then left a trail of it through the entire house ending in *your* bedroom— and on *your* shoes?" (Uh-oh. Busted.)

Not me!

The next level past "Not me!" immaturity is "blaming somebody else." And even though it might feel like you're taking partial responsibility—it's really not much better. Does this sound familiar?

IT'S REALLY NOT MY FAULT! IF YOU'D BEEN LOOKING WHERE YOU WERE WALKING, THEN YOU WOULD HAVE SEEN MY SKATEBOARD ON THE STEPS, NOT TRIPPED ON IT, AND WOULDN'T HAVE ALL THOSE STITCHES AND A BUSTED-UP FACE!

A true sign of growth is being able to *admit* when you make a mistake and *owning* it. It's called "taking responsibility." The funny part is that we all know EVERYBODY messes up, yet it's *still* hard for us to own up to our mistakes. But when we do—it's huge.

Once you learn to Own It, the next step is trying to Make Things Right. Sometimes that involves cleaning something up, fixing something, or apologizing to someone you've hurt.

When you take responsibility for a slipup—and then make it right—it shows you're ready for bigger things. Trust grows. And that sure beats *Not me!*

"TAKING RESPONSIBILITY MEANS MAKING SURE I HAVE ENOUGH TIME TO DO HOMEWORK AND PRACTICE PIANO AND DO WHAT I WANT AFTER SCHOOL."
—CINDY, 7TH GRADE

37. INDIVIDUATION (DIFFERING OPINIONS FROM PARENTS AND FRIENDS)

Okay—what's up with using that huge word in the chapter title? Well, it makes us feel smart when we use a long word. (Just kidding.) Actually, this word describes something that's happening in the middle school years.

You probably remember learning how to break a word into two parts so you could understand it better—so let's do that now. The first part (*individu-*) sounds a lot like *individual*, right? (Or you could say *original*, *unique*, or *one-of-a-kind*.) Then there's *-ation*, which basically means "becoming." So if you're *individuating*, then you're becoming an original.

Sure, you've always been an original in God's eyes. But think about it: From the time you were born, you've pretty much copied whatever you've seen and heard, right? Your first word was probably something like "ma-ma" (influenced by the woman who kept repeating "ma ma ma ma" while you sat in her lap). And copying is how you learned to shove food into your *mouth* instead of, say, your ear because you watched other people cram chow into theirs. So much can be learned by copying other people.

As you get older, copying happens in friendships, too. Part of the reason I listened to the music I listened to in junior high is because everyone else was listening to it. How much "copying" do you see in what other middle schoolers wear, watch, and listen to?

BUT junior high is an amazing time to (here comes that big word again) *INDIVIDUATE* and figure out WHO you really are and WHAT your opinions are—independent of your parents and not exactly like your friends, either.

Why don't people do it sooner? I don't know for sure—because we like safety, maybe? It's not easy to do something *different*, is it? But it's funny how we always admire people who are bold enough to try.

It's really all about learning to think for yourself. Opportunities are all around you:

- People are harassing someone—you can choose not to!

- There's a school club that none of your buddies wants to try—you can do it!

- Your friends burn through their money at the mall—you could save some of yours to help feed hungry people!

Some things are true and unchangeable. But for millions of things, there's not one "right answer." It's up to the Original You!

38. WHAT TO DO WHEN SOMEONE LABELS YOU

Lots of people like to put stuff in categories.

It's helpful, you know? When you want a spoon for your McFlurry, it's cool when the spoons are in the slot labeled Spoons so you don't have to dig through the straws, napkins, and forks. Or if you want mild sauce for your bean burrito, you can make sure you don't grab the one that's marked Burning Hot Volcano Fire Sauce. (That'd be bad.)

But you know, people try to put other people into categories, too. It works fine...sometimes. Maybe you're in the band, in a club, or on a team. You're probably in a certain teacher's classroom. Those are all categories, and they're based on facts. You're either in Mr. Shlumguleon's science class—or you're not.

But sometimes people come up with their own categories that aren't based on facts, and they slap some kind of label on you (or on your friend). Ugh.

Nerd

Sissy

Prude

Spaz

What then?

REALIZE THAT NEGATIVE "LABEL MAKERS" ARE MISTAKEN

God made everyone unique and original (look back at chapter 37). Your *true* label comes from God, your Designer. When you know Jesus as the Leader of your life, here are some *fantastic* labels God places on you:

God's child (John 1:12)

Jesus' friend (John 15:15)

Forgiven (Colossians 1:13-14)

Complete in Christ (Colossians 2:9-10)

A citizen of heaven (Philippians 3:20)

God's workmanship (Ephesians 2:10)

A member of Christ's body (1 Corinthians 12:27)

BE CAREFUL NOT TO BE A "LABEL MAKER"

It's easy to notice what makes people different (especially if they've "labeled" you first). Instead, focus on what makes us all similar.

God is the Master Designer, and God didn't make *any* mistakes when he made each of us. You'll never see a person whom God's not *crazy* about. So even if you don't have something great to say about someone, don't label her with something God didn't intend.

SECTION 5

EMOTIONS

39. WHAT'S HAPPENING WITH MY EMOTIONS?

Have you noticed a change in your emotions?

Do you have days or parts of days or even a few minutes when you feel pumped, but then just the next day (or part of a day or even a few minutes later) you feel really depressed? Have you noticed that sometimes you feel kind of sad for no real reason? Or you have a bunch of red-hot anger, and you're not really sure why? Do you ever have fights with your parents or siblings or friends and afterward think, *Wow, what was* that *all about? Why was I fighting about* that *stupid little thing?*

Welcome to the world of young teenage emotional change. It's a wild roller-coaster ride, baby. So make sure the safety bar is tight across your lap and hold on tight.

Remember that chapter on abstract thinking (chapter 22)? That's what's messing with your emotions right now. See, emotions are all abstract. So when you were a little kid, the emotions you could experience and how you experienced them were limited because your brain couldn't think abstractly.

But NOW—you amazing brainiac!—your brain is ready for wild new emotions. It's also preparing you to experience old emotions in brand-new ways and to greater extremes.

The problem is, you're not used to these new emotions. They feel like a brand-new pair of jeans—stiff and uncomfortable. So while you're trying to get used to them, these unfamiliar emotions are taking you on a wild ride, often confusing you, and making you feel out of control.

Once again, we say this is all normal. In fact, it's massively good. Why? Read the next chapter.

40. WHAT'S "GOOD" ABOUT MY CHANGING EMOTIONS?

When your emotions are all over the place and you feel totally out of control, it's hard to imagine that this change is good.

When you spend days feeling depressed and you don't know why, it's a challenge to think, *Yeah, this is good.*

When you get super angry at the stupidest little things, it's difficult to see how this emotional change can be a gift from God.

But a gift from God is exactly what emotional change is all about.

Read this verse—it's one of our favorites in the whole Bible:

> *I HAVE COME THAT THEY MAY HAVE LIFE, AND HAVE IT TO THE FULL.*
> —JESUS (JOHN 10:10)

Here's the dealio: God absolutely adores you. God loves you perfectly. And one of God's greatest desires is that you'd experience a full and wonderful life. That's the desire Jesus expresses to all of us in John 10:10.

But to really experience a full and wonderful life as an adult, you have to have a full collection of possible emotions. If adults went through life with only the emotions that little kids can experience, then their lives wouldn't be very full or wonderful.

So God, in his perfect design, created this thing you're going through, this occasionally messy change. Because God loves you, God gave you this great gift so you can experience life to the fullest while you're growing up. Make sense?

41. WHY ADULTS MIGHT DOWNPLAY YOUR EMOTIONS

Have you ever been around a little kid who's having a hard time describing his emotions? He might stomp on the ground and make a really serious face; but when you ask him what's wrong, he answers something like, "I don't know! I just feel all...all jumbly inside" (or some other made-up word like that).

A child makes up a word to describe what he's feeling because he doesn't have the vocabulary to make sense of his world. And if he says he feels "jumbly"—or "fizzy" or "squishy" or "soupy" or some other funny word—then, at the *very least*, you'll probably smile. But it's more likely you'll giggle a bit or even laugh right in his face. Meanie!

Put yourself in the kid's shoes and make both people in the example 10 years older. You are yourself (ooh, that's a stretch!), and there's some adult watching you or listening to you deal with your new emotions. She sees you angrily stomping around the kitchen because your favorite cereal is all gone. Or she sees you giggling and whispering with your friends with the kind of excitement that only middle school girls are capable of feeling. Or she sees you moping around all the time, as though the world has come to an end.

Adults don't typically remember very well what it's like to have middle school emotions—feelings that are all over the place and out of control and, well, weird. So when adults hear a middle schooler say, "I'm in love!" most think (or say), *Uh, you don't know what love is yet.* In most cases they're not trying to be mean. They've just forgotten what it's like to be your age. (Hey, we hate to admit it, but sometimes we—Marko and Scott—are just like "them.") Adults don't realize you're experiencing love like you've never felt before—so it's really huge to you!

Yeah, that's why adults sometimes make fun of or downplay teenage emotions. If an adult says something like, "What you're feeling isn't real," you can respond—politely, of course—with, "Well, it's real to me."

42. WHY DO I FEEL SAD ALL THE TIME?

Everybody gets sad.

But sometimes you can feel *waaay* low and be unsure if you can shake it. We'd like to tell you a snappy joke here; but when you're dealing with deep sadness, humor's not the first thing on your mind. (Have you ever had someone try to "help you out" when you're really sad by trying to make you laugh? Yep, we have, too. It's not so funny sometimes.)

Here are some things to keep in mind when the waves of sadness come crashing onto your shore:

YOU'RE STILL NORMAL

Well...whatever "normal" is. Not only can those famous hormones make things more challenging, but it's all part of your brain "growing up" and learning how to process sadness. Some days are just *hard*; there's no way to sugarcoat it and no magic wand to wave around and change things. But don't give up. Sadness is one natural part of this crazy life we live, but it's not the whole thing. Not only that, but it's something you *can* learn to deal with.

"ALONE-NESS"

When you're sad, being alone can be good sometimes—even though it can *feel* bad. Getting alone to think can really help when you're sad. It can help you think about what's real. Because—truth is—even when you're alone, you're not *really* alone. God is there with you, ready to listen and to give you strength. Try talking to God about how you feel.

However, keep in mind that *too* much time alone can sometimes make sadness feel more intense, and you can end up feeling isolated. This leads us to a final (and important) thought:

TALK TO SOMEONE

Your emotions can help you see what's going on deep inside you. Maybe your sadness has been an everyday thing for a long time now. If you feel so sad you just can't deal with it and aren't sure you'll be able to shake the feeling, then you've gotta tell somebody. You're still "normal" (there's that word again), but everybody needs help sometimes—and right now might be *your* time. Think of the adult who cares most about you, take a deep breath, and go talk to her. You'll be so glad you did.

> "LOTS OF PEOPLE CAN FEEL DEPRESSED WHEN THEY'RE YOUNG, BUT MY UNCLE ALWAYS TOLD ME TO BOTTLE THE POSITIVE AND WORK ON THE NEGATIVE."
>
> —NICK, 8TH GRADE

43. WHERE'S ALL THIS ANGER COMING FROM?

Ever been mad? No, I mean REALLY mad!

I remember times my parents would ground me for something I did. (It happened a lot, actually.) I'd get SO furious—the kind of mad that you can feel all over your body. The kind of mad where you want to shoot lightning bolts out of your eyeballs and destroy things. The kind of mad where cartoon characters blow smoke out of their ears.

Have you ever been *that* mad? We have!

WHAT MAKES YOU ANGRY?

Anger is sometimes called a "secondary emotion." Huh? That simply means that lots of times anger is actually a *reaction* to another core feeling that might not be as easy for you to express. Detecting what's *causing* the anger is a big deal. You might actually be feeling hurt or scared or sad, but it comes out as anger.

Did you ever meet someone who seemed really mad all the time? Imagine you found out that—

- his parents just got divorced, or

- her favorite uncle died, or

- he got cut from the team he'd always dreamed about making.

Instead of coming out as sadness, the person's feelings came out as anger.

When you're in middle school, a part of your "growing up" (like we talked about in section 4) is learning to figure out where your anger's coming from. Sometimes that's pretty hard to do—but it's definitely possible. (And it's even more possible if you're willing to get quiet with God and see what he might want to tell you.)

IS ANGER ALWAYS "BAD"?

The short answer? No way! Sometimes God *uses* our anger to help make wrong stuff right. In Matthew 21:12, we read how Jesus was so mad that he flipped over some tables in the temple. Yep, even Jesus got angry—for the right reasons. (Look it up.)

You may have seen someone being treated unfairly, and it made you SO mad. Your *anger* can spur you to *action*—to stick up for someone, defend someone, or correct something that's wrong. When that happens, anger's actually a gift that will help you—and maybe even others.

"DON'T TAKE YOUR ANGER OUT ON OTHER PEOPLE."

—AARON, 7TH GRADE

44. CAN EMOTIONS BE CONTROLLED?

Over the years that we've worked with young teenagers, we've heard hundreds of parents and older people in the church say something like, "You need to teach those kids to control their emotions."

Our response is usually, "Well, at this point in their lives, I'd rather they learn to *understand* their emotions than to *control* their emotions."

Really, it's much more important that you grow in your understanding of what you're feeling and experiencing. Typically the people who say that to us are really saying (or thinking), "You need to teach those kids to express their emotions in a way that I'm comfortable with."

You really do make older people uncomfortable, you know. They look at you and think, *A live explosive! I'm gonna die!* (Okay, we're kidding—but only a little bit.)

That said, there's a time and a place for the *expression* of your emotions, right? You can't make yourself *not* feel something, but you sure have a choice about how you express that emotion and how far you allow the emotion to take you. For instance, most people don't start shouting about how angry they are in the middle of a crowded movie theater. And if you're out for a fancy dinner and the dessert makes you extremely happy, then you probably won't choose to skip around the entire restaurant shouting, "I'm so happy! I'm so happy! Who wants to taste my dessert?"

So, yes, there's some truth to the idea that you can, and should, control your emotions. But people who control their emotions *too much* end up depressed, physically sick, and in relational trouble. Seriously— stuffing your emotions (ignoring them) is massively unhealthy.

The trick is to learn how to notice your emotions so they don't control you. When you feel a sudden burst of anger, think to yourself, *Ooh, I'm feeling angry. Hello, anger. Pretty ticked, aren't you?* Once you've noticed the emotion (and really, that's a big part of maturity), then you can think about how to appropriately express it, which is different from "controlling" it.

45. DRAMA

ADJUSTING HIS TOUGH-GUY FOOTBALL JERSEY, HE INHALES A LARGE BREATH OF AIR, DIGS DEEP FOR SOME COURAGE, AND WALKS STRAIGHT TOWARD HER LOCKER. HE TRIES TO REMAIN COOL, EVEN WHEN HE ALMOST TRIPS OVER HER BOOKS SITTING ON THE FLOOR. SHE STANDS THERE IN HER SPIFFY CHEERLEADING OUTFIT, LOOKING PROUD AND SASSY. HE SPEAKS ONLY A FEW WORDS, BUT HER FACE IMMEDIATELY TURNS SOUR. SHE SPINS AWAY AND SLAMS HER LOCKER DOOR, BARK-ING A FEW SHARP WORDS OVER HER SHOULDER AND NOT REALIZING THAT HER POM-POMS ARE STUCK IN THE LOCKER DOOR. THE STUDENTS STANDING NEARBY CAN'T HEAR WHAT SHE SAID, BUT THEY START TO WHISPER ABOUT WHAT JUST HAPPENED…OH, THE DRAMA OF IT ALL!

Middle school life and drama—they go together at times, don't they? Dripping with emotion, super-charged with conflict, usually intense, and often unpredictable. Why is it like this? Well, life is com-plicated, tough to figure out, and oozing with ups and downs. But hey, that's part of what makes it interesting, too.

Do you know what a "drama" is? It's a *per-formance*. When you're performing, you're doing something for an audience. Do you know people who seem to live for the response of the "audience" around them, instead of thinking through the best (most mature) choices?

I (Scott) had a friend in school named Erika. She was a great girl. She was also an actress. She had big parts in the school plays, and she was great on the stage. The problem was that sometimes Erika seemed to forget that her whole life wasn't a stage.

Many of her words and actions looked like a constant "show" for the people around her. (Except nobody could edit the parts that should've been placed on the gag reel.)

It doesn't take a "theater person" to get caught up in the drama cycle, though. It's easy to watch any one of those hour-long TV shows overflowing with crisis, excitement, and buzz, and believe that's "reality." But reality includes thinking, sleeping, time alone, bathroom stops, waiting for stuff, and many other "regular moments"—none of which makes for very good TV drama.

Yes, life has moments that are dramatic, emotional, and challenging—but your life's not a performance to entertain the people around you. However, there IS an audience of One that matters—*God*! God is tuned in to your life continuously, cheering for you, crying during sad moments, and wanting you to live out the adventure designed for you.

Next time you crave the spotlight, remember to "perform" for the right Audience. (Or sign up for a part in the school play.)

"SAVE THE DRAMA FOR YOUR MAMA."
—CASIE AND LAUREN, 8TH GRADE

46. INTENSITY

Intensity. What does that word mean?

Extremeness. Concentration. Passion. Focus. Strength.

Have you ever felt intensity?

We thought so. We have, too.

You can feel intense emotions lots of times in life, but having strong feelings about stuff can be HUGE during your middle school years. But catch this: Intensity can be both a friend and an enemy.

ON THE (+) SIDE: INTENSITY CAN LEAD TO *ACTION*. Think of a cartoon character you like: Sponge-Bob, The Powerpuff Girls, even Bugs Bunny. When they're *really* angry, smoke comes out of their ears. Or when they're *really* feeling love, huge red hearts pop into the air all around them. But what happens next? They DO something! They chase somebody, whack somebody with a club, throw somebody off a cliff, or twist somebody up in a knot (sometimes this happens whether they're feeling love or anger). That's when intensity is a gift—because it gets us off the couch and into the game.

I (Scott) know a seventh-grade girl who was feeling intense sadness about the fact that so many villages in Africa don't have clean water and people are needlessly dying from diseases as a result. But instead of just feeling sad, she let her intensity move her to ACTION! For her last birthday, this girl asked her parents and friends not to get her any gifts, but to donate the money they *would* have spent on her gifts to an organization that's building clean water wells in those African villages. Intense! And intensely good.

ON THE (-) SIDE: INTENSITY CAN LEAD TO *WORRY AND STRESS.*

Sometimes intensity can be a negative. Especially when we keep it inside and believe it's up to us to handle everything. Part of the challenge of having intense emotions is deciding when it's supposed to prompt us to ACTION and when we just need to relax, breathe deeply, and take a chill pill. In Luke 12:25 Jesus says, "Who of you by worrying can add a single hour to your life?" Nobody can. Talking to God and to godly people about your worries can help. Intensity is worse when you're dealing with it alone. (Check out the next chapter for more about that.)

So the next time something's feeling "intense" to you, ask God to show you if there's an action you need to take, someone you need to talk to—or a combination of the two. It's way better than having smoke come out of your ears.

47. LONELINESS

"ONE IS THE LONELIEST NUMBER…"

—*FROM "ONE," A SONG BY A REALLY OLD BAND CALLED THREE DOG NIGHT*

For years people have written songs about being lonely. I looked online and found a list of 398 songs about loneliness. Man, if those songwriters were really so lonely, maybe they should have stopped writing songs and hung out together instead! But it's not always that easy, is it?

Do you ever wonder why loneliness can feel so bad? God built us to be in relationships—it's how we're designed.

Most people believe the first problem for humanity happened when sin entered the world, but it's not true. When God was creating the world, at the end of every day, God said, "That's *good*." But one day, before sin came upon the scene, God said—

IT IS NOT GOOD *FOR THE MAN TO BE ALONE.*

—GENESIS 2:18 (EMPHASIS ADDED)

The first "not good" of creation. But God solved Adam's aloneness by creating Eve. God knew Adam and Eve *needed each other* so they could help each other and form a bond and experience intimacy.

One "loneliness buster" you can try is simply taking a risk and pursuing a friendship. We know it's not easy; but don't forget that lots of people are feeling lonely and are just waiting for someone to start a conversation with them. (Hey, maybe they're even writing songs about it!)

I (Scott) remember when my parents dropped me off at college for the first time. I didn't know anybody there, and I sat alone in my dorm room for about a half-hour, feeling REALLY sad. Then I wondered how many other new freshmen were sitting in their dorm rooms alone like me. With nothing to lose, I grabbed a football, started knocking on doors, and asked if anyone wanted to be lonely together. About an hour later, I laughed to myself as more than a dozen guys played a hilarious football game—and none of us knew each other before that afternoon. I became really good friends with some of them, but it all started with my taking a risk. I'm glad I did.

Sometimes we'll feel lonely even when other people are around. But remember that once you begin a friendship with Jesus, you're *never* really alone. The first Bible verse I memorized was Joshua 1:9—

HAVE I NOT COMMANDED YOU? BE STRONG AND COURAGEOUS. DO NOT BE AFRAID; DO NOT BE DISCOURAGED, FOR THE LORD YOUR GOD WILL BE WITH YOU WHEREVER YOU GO.

Loneliness happens. More songs will be written about it, for sure. But even when you're lonely...God won't leave you alone.

"HOW DO THE 'RIGHT' PEOPLE MANAGE TO OSTRACIZE EVERYONE?"
—ZACH, 8TH GRADE

48. MY FRIENDS' EMOTIONS

Okay, so not only do you have to figure out *your own* emotions, but you also have friends who're trying to figure out *their* emotions. Here are a couple of things to remember:

BE CAREFUL NOT TO JUDGE SOMEONE'S EMOTIONS AS "RIGHT" OR "WRONG."

How someone feels is really up to that person and nobody else—which is a good thing. You probably wouldn't like it if someone told you how you should feel. No matter how well you know people, you can't know everything that's going on with them. Let's say your friend's dog dies, and your friend is sad—for weeks! You might be thinking, *Get over it already!* But even if you've gone through the loss of a pet before, you still can't feel *exactly* what your friend is feeling. Maybe there's some information you don't know—like all the time he spent with that dog while his parents were splitting up. Or maybe it's not something he can explain; it's just how this new situation hit him, and his feelings can't be helped or "figured out." Regardless of whether or not you understand your friends' feelings, you can still respond with prayer and Christ-like love.

REALIZE YOU CAN'T "CHANGE" YOUR FRIENDS' EMOTIONS.

When you see someone in a tough place, you want to help him feel better. But a person needs to process his emotions at his own pace. Let's say that instead of your friend's dog dying, he loses a parent or a grandparent, or maybe his parents divorce. You probably wouldn't "judge" his emotions, but you'd sure like to take away his sadness. Yet, as crazy as it might seem, even tough emotions like sadness are gifts from God. Your friend's emotions could be exactly what God wants him to experience right now so he can process through them and grow. Don't try to change your friends' feelings—just care about how your friends feel.

HOW A FRIEND HANDLES HER EMOTIONS TELLS YOU A LOT ABOUT WHAT KIND OF FRIEND SHE IS.

Pay attention to how your friend deals with her feelings. If you have a friend who "needs to get revenge" when she's hurt, think about how she'd treat you if you got on her bad side. You must choose your friends wisely.

IF YOU'RE REALLY WORRIED ABOUT HOW YOUR FRIEND IS HANDLING HER EMOTIONS, TALK TO HER. AND TALK TO SOMEONE ELSE, TOO.

How your friend deals with her feelings may worry you—and that's a sign of being a good friend. But if you worry that your friend's sadness or anger might cause her to hurt either herself or someone else, then it's time to talk to an adult about it. Ask a trustworthy adult for help. Sometimes our emotions can overwhelm us, and the best thing a friend can do is to let somebody know.

I WAS A MIDDLE SCHOOL DORK!
—SCOTT

When I was in middle school, it seemed as if my parents had way too many rules for me. But because it was their house, and because they often repeated the dreaded "Because I said so" proclamation, I was usually left with little choice. I had to obey their rules.

So sometimes, when my parents went out, I'd take some gambles with the rules. And I usually lost.

If you were to ask any of my three siblings, they'd tell you that I was the one who got in trouble the most. (I'm not sure if I was actually the worst behaved or if I just got busted the most.) And when I got in trouble, one of the first things my parents took away was my TV-watching time. But when my parents went out, I usually thought, *How will they know if I sneak a little TV time?*

I'll tell you how they'd know. Our TV was pretty old. It worked fine, but after it had been turned on for a while, the whole set would feel warm to the touch. So when my parents returned from wherever they'd been, the first thing my mom would do is walk over to the TV set (can you tell she didn't trust me?) and put her hand on top. This way she instantly knew if I'd been watching TV when I wasn't supposed to.

One night I got an idea for how to beat the "warm TV." My parents were out, and I wanted to sneak some TV time. So I went to the freezer and filled a plastic bag with ice cubes. I brought the bag over by the television and started watching *The Six Million Dollar Man*. As soon as I heard the garage door opening, I turned off the show, set the bag of ice on top of the TV for about 20 or 30 seconds, and then dashed into the next room, pitching the ice down the sink.

Sure enough, Mom walked in the house and headed for the TV. But this time when she put her hand on it, she scrunched her eyebrows down (you know how parents do that?) and looked doubtful.

She said, "Hey, Scott? Do you have any idea why the TV set is FREEZING COLD?"

Thinking quickly, I said, "I don't know...I guess no one's been watching it for a *reeeeally* long time."

I bet you're not surprised to learn it was quite a while before I watched *The Six Million Dollar Man* again.

SECTION 6

FAITH
CHANGES

49. WHAT'S CHANGING?

Has this ever happened to you? You're cruising through life, not thinking much about anything, feeling pretty good about God and stuff, when suddenly—

Duh-duh-duh! (imagine some scary music)

—you start to think that maybe—just maybe—what you've believed about something for the last several years might not be completely true.

That can be a bit freaky. But truthfully, when you get used to this kind of feeling, it can be really cool. We (Marko and Scott) love discovering we haven't believed or understood something quite right because that means we get to move toward a new and better understanding or belief!

But when you first start to experience this shift, it can be disturbing. Like, what if you've always believed that God will give you whatever you pray for as long as it isn't selfish, or something like that? Now imagine your favorite relative is really sick with cancer, and you've been praying hard for her healing. You really believe she'll get better, but then she dies. Now you're probably thinking, *So why do I even pray?*

What's changed? Well, do you remember reading the section of this book on how your brain is changing (section 3), and especially that super-important chapter on abstract thinking (chapter 22)? That's changing your faith, too. Now that your brain is working differently—more like an adult's brain than a kid's brain—the abstract stuff of faith needs to be rethought. It's almost like you need to reboot your belief.

Some of this happens naturally, but there's a risk, too. Lots of teenagers end up either chucking their faith or walking away from it slowly. That's because they don't do the hard work of rethinking their faith using their new brainpower. And because they don't rethink their faith, they move into their older teenage years with a little kid's faith—or no faith at all.

We promise you this: Little-kid faith just doesn't cut it when you're 18.

50. FROM CHILDHOOD FAITH TO TEENAGE FAITH

We're writing this book—actually, we're typing it on a keyboard—with our laptop computers. Our computers each have an "operating system." (Have you learned about this in school?) The operating system works with all the computer's programs to help it "think" a certain way. Maybe you've used a PC computer with a "Windows" operating system. Or maybe you've used an Apple computer with its OS operating system. (Duh, OS stands for "operating system"!)

Once in a while, Microsoft or Apple will come out with new operating systems, and everyone eventually updates their computers. But there's still some stuff that was created using an older operating system saved on our computers, and when we open one of those old files, the computer quickly "converts" it to the new system. Then if we make some changes to it, a question pops up: "Do you want to save this in the new format or the old format?"

That's exactly what's happening in your faith as you move from childhood to adulthood. You're going through life, minding your own business, believing what you believe, when one of the things you've always believed suddenly doesn't make sense anymore (like the example in the last chapter about a favorite relative dying even though you prayed for her). You have three choices at that point:

1. Say to yourself, *Well, this doesn't work,* and throw it away—choosing not to believe it anymore.

2. Say to yourself, *Ah, this belief doesn't make sense, but it's all I've got,* and move toward adulthood with a little kid's faith.

3. Say to yourself, *Ooh, this is going to be hard work, but I have to figure out how to re-think this belief in a way that makes sense.*

Option 3—yeah, that's what we're hoping you'll do. Actually, option 3 is why we're writing these books. We want to *help* you rethink your faith.

Three cheers for new operating systems: Woo hoo! Woo hoo! Woo hoo!

51. DOUBT

As a little kid, you probably believed most of the stuff your parents told you. And that's a good thing.

But at some point, you may have started wondering if everything you'd ever been told was true. If not, and you're still hiding lost teeth under your pillow, then skip over these next few sentences.

I (Scott) remember when I realized there was enough evidence to make me doubt that a fairy was coming into my bedroom and exchanging money for molars. Honestly, my next thought was about Santa and the Egg-Delivering Bunny, but the next *doubt* that entered my mind was about God.

I'd never actually seen the fairy or the rabbit, and I'd never actually had a look at God, either. Was it safe—or even "right"—to doubt whether God was real? Absolutely. And we (Marko and Scott) believe that when you face your doubts head-on, it actually helps your journey of faith. When you question something, it leads you on a search for what's true. And that's good!

Admitting your doubts is different than being *frozen* by your doubt. We need to be honest about our doubts and ask God to help us through them. **Honesty** is the key here.

There was a man living in Jesus' time whose son was possessed by demons. The son was unable to speak, and he would even foam at the mouth and roll around on the ground—sounds pretty gnarly.

(Check out the story in Mark 9:14-29.) The boy's dad went to ask Jesus if he could help his son, and Jesus told the man, "Everything is possible for one who believes" (verse 23). The father's response to Jesus (verse 24) was pretty honest:

"I DO BELIEVE; HELP ME OVERCOME MY UNBELIEF!"

The first time I read that, I thought, *So did he believe...or not?* Well, now I trust the Bible is saying the man believed it was possible for Jesus to help—*even while he had doubts.* How do you think Jesus reacted to the man's request for help in overcoming his doubts? Was Jesus ticked the guy couldn't just "have faith"? That's what I figured when I first read it. But I was wrong. Jesus *did* heal the man's son. And I believe it was at least partly because Jesus was glad the man chose to be honest with him, instead of trying to "fake his faith." I bet that guy's faith was way stronger afterward—especially since he'd been *honest* about his doubts.

What doubts do you have? Are you willing to be open and truthful about 'em? You'll be glad you did. *Undoubtedly!*

52. WHAT TO DO WITH QUESTIONS?

The first thing you need to do when you have questions about your faith is...congratulate yourself!

Huh?

We mean it. When you have questions about your faith, that means your brain is turned on, and you're really considering this amazing God and all that he's about. That's already a big win.

Marko and I both have families. When our kids were little, we told them about God. We told them God loved them, and they believed us even though they couldn't see God. Maybe your parents told you the same thing when you were little. We probably could have told our kids a gigantic pink elephant was out there somewhere, and that even though they couldn't see it, this elephant loved them. They probably would've believed it...for a while. But sooner or later, they'd have had some big questions—questions that couldn't get answered because the invisible pink elephant doesn't exist.

But God *does* exist, and God isn't afraid of your questions. In fact, God invites them. God doesn't want you to shut off your brain and just blindly trust. God wants you to ask your questions, and God wants to help you answer them, too. Here are hints:

GET A BIBLE THAT'S RIGHT FOR YOU.

Do you have a Bible of your own? If you do, then does it have more pictures than words? That picture Bible might have been good enough when you were little, but now you need a Bible that will help you answer more mature questions. Lots of Bibles have a topical index in the back where you can look up specific areas related to your questions and it'll point you to where the Bible talks about that topic. There are also great Bibles with "study notes" written right next to the Scripture text. Those notes are different from the actual God-inspired Bible—they're just somebody's thoughts about the passage. But they can often answer a bunch of the questions you have.

GET GUTSY AND ASK AN ADULT YOU TRUST.

Sometimes students don't ask their questions because they think they're "dumb questions." We've *all* had questions like that. But we (Marko and Scott) both LOVE IT when middle schoolers are bold enough to ask questions about God or their faith. Even though we don't know every answer, we love to help students figure it out.

GET INTO A CHURCH OR YOUTH GROUP WHERE YOU CAN KEEP LAUNCHING YOUR QUESTIONS.

Hopefully your questions will keep on coming because that means you're *growing* in your faith. If you don't have a good youth group where you can keep figuring stuff out, *please* find one. Check with your friends who seem to learn stuff about God at their churches—and go together. Learning with a buddy can be fun, and you can encourage each other along the way.

RELATIONSHIP CHANGES

53. WHY ARE MY FRIENDSHIPS CHANGING?

Think about the first friends you had when you were a little kid. (Maybe some of those people are still your friends today. Or maybe not.) Before you started school, chances are the kids you spent time with were simply the children of people your mom or dad hung out with. And that's cool because most little kids get along. You don't hear them saying, "Brittany has a nicer highchair than I do" or "Jake's way into Legos, and I'm more into choo-choo trains...so we don't hang out."

But friendships—like everything else we've been talking about in this book—CHANGE over time, don't they? But *why*? Why can't we just stay in the tight little circle of kids we shared animal crackers with at preschool? Here are a couple of reasons:

YOUR CHARACTER AND PERSONALITY ARE GROWING AND CHANGING—AND SO ARE YOUR FRIENDS'.
You're becoming a different person than you were when you were little—and your friends are, too. Sometimes your friendships will grow tighter as you get older because you're growing and changing in similar ways. But other times, you'll grow in different ways. As your tastes and preferences get more defined, you might find they're definitely different from a friend's who you used to feel pretty similar to. Now that doesn't have to end a friendship, but it can change it a little—or a lot.

THE "RATE" AT WHICH YOU'RE GROWING AND CHANGING IS DIFFERENT FROM YOUR FRIENDS'.

So what, you say? There's nothing wrong with growing and changing at different speeds, right? True, but you may find yourself trying to deal with things your friend doesn't have to face yet. For instance, let's say your body is hitting some of the crazy changes that puberty brings (you know, all the physical stuff we talked about in section 2). And suppose you've got a friend who's not dealing with *any* of those changes yet. You may still be friends with him, but your "shared experience" might make your friendship feel different than it used to.

Remember, just because your friendships might "change" doesn't mean they have to *end*. In fact, those friends can be some of the greatest pals of all—people who've known you for a long time and who can give you a different perspective on things as they're growing and changing, too.

"I'M SAD TO LEAVE MY OLD FRIENDSHIPS, BUT GLAD FOR NEW ONES."

—ROBYN, 7TH GRADE

54. LEAVING ELEMENTARY SCHOOL FRIENDS BEHIND?

Think for a minute about the friends you had in first grade. Can you remember any of them? Who was sitting next to you when you were learning to print your name, tell time, and write your numbers? Those were good days, huh? (Bet you had less homework then.)

Time moves on, though, and you get older. Your friends get older, too. The kid who told you jokes as you learned your multiplication tables isn't part of the group you hang out with now. And when you get to middle school, it's pretty much unavoidable that you'll leave most of your elementary school friends behind, right?

Wait a minute...not so fast. It doesn't *have* to be that way.

Sure, you'll meet new people and have more chances for new friendships throughout middle school. But instead of turning your back on your fourth-grade buddies, what if you could keep the old friends while you still make new ones? It IS possible. And don't let anyone tell you it's not.

Even though some of your new middle school friends might share more of your interests than your elementary school friends do, don't toss the old friendships onto the garbage pile too soon. It's not like you can fit only a certain number of friends into your "friend space" and then it's full. Why not *expand* your circle of friends instead of trading out old ones for new ones? It'll take a little work to keep in touch with the people you don't see as often—but really, how much effort does a phone call, text, or trip to Starbucks take? Not a lot.

A bonus to keeping old friendships is the "guy-girl factor." It's almost like having a brother or sister in the same grade who helps you out. Remember back in kindergarten when you played with boys or girls only, never giving much thought to the whole guy-girl thing? Guys, some of those girls you've been friends with since elementary school can be a big help when you're trying to understand more about that new girl you're crushing on. And girls, it's cool to have an "old" guy friend looking out for you when you're meeting new guys.

So if you haven't been paying much attention to that friend from the good ol' days of learning how many pennies are in a dime, then go ahead and restart the conversation. You'll be glad you did—and they'll probably be glad, too.

55. GUY CRAZY/GIRL CRAZY

BODY FACT: IN AN AVERAGE LIFETIME, A PERSON WILL WALK ABOUT 115,000 MILES—OR MORE THAN FOUR TIMES AROUND THE EARTH AT THE EQUATOR.

This is one of the most interesting changes that occur during the middle school years. Wasn't it just yesterday you believed members of the opposite sex had *cooties*? And when you joked with your friends about having boyfriends or girlfriends, they were always quick to say, "NO WAY!" But then...slowly...the opposite sex didn't look quite as gross as it used to, huh? How did this happen? Did the Puberty Fairy wave a magic wand or what?

Almost every class has one (maybe it's YOU!)—someone who *loves* talking about the opposite sex. It's the girl who draws a boy's initials on her folders and sketches hearts in her notebooks. It's the guy who gets his buddies to walk past the girls again... and again, and he always seems to have a crush on one of them.

Did you know this whole idea of guy-girl attraction is actually God's invention? Yep—God built our hearts to enjoy relationships with the opposite sex. And the middle school years are when you discover just how COOL it can feel.

It's kinda like when I (Scott) took my son trick-or-treating for the first time. Sure, he thought the Buzz Lightyear costume looked cool, but he had no idea what it was really all about. When he toddled up to the first house and received some candy just for ringing the doorbell, he looked at me wide-eyed as if to say, "This is amazing!" That's a little like how it feels when you start exploring the world of the opposite sex.

However, there's a trap in this "guy crazy/girl crazy" deal. Some teenagers start believing they won't be worth much until (or unless) they have boyfriends or girlfriends. We've seen students get stuck in that way of thinking, to the point where they're just obsessing about their crushes. And that's not good. Your value is not (not, not, not!) determined by whether or not you have a boyfriend or girlfriend. And it never will be.

Maybe you're reading this and thinking, *I'm NOT guy crazy or girl crazy, and thinking about the opposite sex isn't anywhere near my radar.* But if a bunch of your friends are, then you might be wondering if you're even on the right schedule. Just as we grow taller at different rates, this "attraction" part of us grows at different rates, too. We know it can be rough if some of your friends are caught up in the chase. But just let 'em do it. As long as they still hang out with you and talk about things besides boys or girls, you can still have great friendships with them. (And when you start to crush on somebody someday, they might be able to give you some tips.)

Oh, and the Puberty Fairy? We were just kidding.

56. INDEPENDENCE

There's one thing we hear from junior highers all the time: "Why can't I have more independence?" We all want more of it, don't we? Well, we've got a tip that can be the key to getting more independence. (Are you excited?)

First, a question: Who has the most control over you? (Right—it's your parents.) Have you ever thought (or said): *I wish my parents would stop treating me like a little kid.* We've heard you say it, and it makes sense.

You probably already know your parents are supposed to help you. (Even when it sometimes doesn't feel like that's what they're doing.) That's their job, and they've been doing it since you were born. For instance, when you were little, your parents wouldn't let you go into the bathroom alone because they thought you might drink the toilet water or something. And they wouldn't let you go outside alone because they knew you'd probably try to play in traffic. There were all kinds of things they wouldn't let you do *because you hadn't proved to them you could handle it.* But now you have. (Cuz we're pretty sure most of you go to the bathroom on your own, right?)

Are you ready to learn The Parent Secret? (We're parents, so we know their secrets.) The key is proving you can handle it. So if you show responsibility, then that will gain you more independence.

But it's not just doing what your parents tell you to do; it's more about your *attitude* when you're doing it. Easier said than done, isn't it? Your parents ask you to take out the trash and recycling. You do it—but with a grumbling, complaining, mumbling-under-your-breath attitude. Well, *that's* not going to get you much. Your parents watch how you handle taking out the trash (or whatever responsibility they give you), and it's a direct indicator to them about how ready you are for more independence. Get it?

So the next time you're thinking about keeping your room clean, doing your homework, or taking out the trash, just remember that if you can actually DO it well and without beefing about it, then you'll be taking some serious steps toward more independence. (Just don't tell your parents that we let you in on The Parent Secret!)

"INDEPENDENCE MAKES ME THINK OF BEING ALONE."
—BLAKE, 7TH GRADE

57. MY CHANGING RELATIONSHIP WITH MY PARENTS

Most likely your parents knew you from the time you were small. Think about it: When they met you, you were probably shorter than two feet tall and weighed less than 12 pounds. You've come a long way, baby!

As *you* change, the way your parents interact with you also changes. Or at least it should. (Check out the last chapter if you think it's not changing fast enough.) It's not always easy to cope with this changing relationship, but did you know you can affect how it goes? It's not all up to you, but you can have more of an effect than you think.

JUST LIKE YOU'RE ENTERING NEW STAGES OF DEVELOPMENT, YOUR MOM AND DAD ARE BOTH LEARNING HOW TO PARENT YOU DURING THOSE STAGES, TOO.
Every school year you have to get used to new classes, new classrooms, new teachers—pretty much a whole new way of doing things, right? Then just when you've figured it out, you move to the next grade and have all new stuff to figure out. Well, believe it or not, your parents have to keep learning a whole new way of doing things, too.

Being Mom or Dad to "toddler you" was way different than being Mom or Dad to "third-grader you." And now that you're in middle school, your parents are learning yet another level of parenting. (This is true even if you have an older brother or sister, because every child is different.) But there's no parent-orientation course called "How Not to Be a Stupid Parent." But you can help them find their way. One way is to...

BE HONEST (AND GENTLE) WHEN YOU FEEL LIKE YOUR PARENTS AREN'T ADJUSTING WELL TO HOW YOU'RE CHANGING.

Think for a minute about how you like to be corrected. If someone notices you could be doing something better and yells, "You're so STUPID! I HATE you!" how would you respond? Probably NOT well. But that's how we've heard lots of kids talk to their parents. Um, we're thinking that's probably *not* going to get those kids what they want.

Instead, what about saying to your parents, "I'd really like to talk to you about some stuff I've been thinking about. When could we do that?" Then, when neither side is angry or in a bad mood, calmly tell your parents what's frustrating you. You didn't have the maturity to talk to your parents this way when you were younger—but you do now.

Have you ever had a conversation with your mom or dad about how being your parent today is different than it was when you were small? Consider asking them, "What's the biggest difference in parenting me now, compared with a few years ago?" You could have a talk that changes things in ways you've never imagined.

"MY PARENTS ARE ANNOYING SOMETIMES AND EMBARRASSING."
—JAYNA, 8TH GRADE

58. MY CHANGING RELATIONSHIP WITH MY CHURCH

One of my (Scott) earliest memories of the church is playing a game of tag in the Sunday school rooms with some buddies. I remember blitzing across the room, avoiding the outstretched hand of "It," and tripping over something. My entire body launched face-first into a concrete wall, knocking out one of my front teeth. Pretty impressive, huh?

At that point in my life, church was just a place where I tried to keep myself entertained and out of trouble. (As you can see, I was at least good at one of the two!) But as we get older, God has designed us to have a much more exciting relationship with the church than just "showing up." And that's a shocker to lots of people. (To be honest, this is a secret that lots of *adults* seem to have missed. I know many junior highers who have this figured out, and they're actually great examples to grown men and women in our church.)

What we're talking about is the move to being a "player" in the church, rather than just a "spectator." It's about *getting into the game* (a way-better game than teeth-smashing-tag). When you realize God is crazy about you, you understand that knowing God isn't just about getting a "free ticket to heaven." There's way more to it than that. God has invited you into this adventure of living—into the excitement of pointing people toward God, serving God's people, and learning more about God's world.

Have you figured out that God has invited you out of the bleachers and onto the field? God made you to be a Player, not a Spectator. And the coolest part is that God made you unique and able to contribute to your church in ways you'll actually love.

EACH OF YOU SHOULD USE WHATEVER GIFT YOU HAVE RECEIVED TO SERVE OTHERS, AS FAITHFUL STEWARDS OF GOD'S GRACE IN ITS VARIOUS FORMS.

—1 PETER 4:10

What kinds of gifts or interests or skills has God given you that you could use in the church? Do you love little kids? You could help in the kids' ministry. Okay, maybe you can't stand little kids, but you love to be outside. Could you help take care of the church— landscaping, mowing, or planting flowers? Or do you have a heart for older people? You could bring so much hope to those who might be struggling with their health or loneliness or depression. There are LOTS more ways to play a part in God's church. What's a way that would fire *you* up? What do you love to do?

The church really does come *alive* when you get out of the grandstand and figure out your position on the field. For me, it's been way more fun than a game of tag.

"MY CHURCH IS A GETAWAY FROM THE OUTSIDE WORLD."

—BRITTANY, 8TH GRADE

59. INTROVERTS AND EXTROVERTS— DIFFERENT RELATIONAL NEEDS

Relationships, friendships, buddies, and pals. As you get older, you realize different people "do friendship" in different ways.

Do you have any "loud friends"? We do. (Lots of them, actually. Some really loud ones!)

Do you have any "quiet friends"? We do, too.

Which one is the "right" kind of friend?

We hope you said, "Neither." But the best kind of friend is one who *understands* that people are different in how they relate to others—and can adjust to it.

Maybe you've heard the words *introvert* and *extrovert* before. Again, there's not a right or a wrong here, just two different approaches to dealing with people who're really worth understanding.

An extrovert is someone who "gets energized by being around people." When given the choice, extroverts will usually choose having a conversation with someone instead of being alone. If an extrovert is alone for too long, he'll go looking for people. Large groups and social places are exciting for extroverts because they're usually ready for a good party—birthday, Christmas, Groundhog Day, "The-Sun's-Out-Today"—any excuse to be with people is fine with them. Do you know anyone like that?

An introvert is someone who "gets energized by being alone"—not all the time, but if they're around people for long stretches, then introverts are likely to need some time by themselves to recharge. It isn't the same thing as being shy, although an introvert might be shy. And an introvert doesn't necessarily have any fear or difficulty about being in social situations. They just really value their "alone time" and need it for refueling.

Most people aren't pure introvert or pure extrovert. Some people find themselves closer to the middle. Or you might be 80 percent extroverted, but still need 20 percent of your time to think on your own. We don't want to make it sound like a math formula. It's more a part of your personality that can't be measured—which is kinda cool.

While you're thinking about which type you are, there's one more thing of importance to keep in mind: *Don't* try to be what you're not. Since there's no introvert/extrovert combination that's the "right" one, just welcome your personality type and get the most out of it that you can.

You should also welcome and accept the personality types of your friends, your parents, and your siblings. If theirs is different from yours, that's cool. Give them freedom to be who God made them to be.

60. A CHANGE IN HOW I CHOOSE FRIENDS

We're going to teach you two big words in this little chapter. Ready? The first one is *proximity* (say prock-SIM-i-tee). The second is *affinity* (say uh-FIN-i-tee).

Most young teenagers go through a major shift in how they choose their friends. You may have noticed that you don't really like to hang out with the same friends you did throughout most of your elementary school days. In fact, this can be a bit confusing—even frustrating.

Your mom might say, "Why don't you hang out with Billy anymore? He's such a nice boy, and he was your friend for so long." You think, *Yeah, but Billy's the biggest dork in school, and we have* nothing *in common anymore!*

It all goes back to that abstract thinking we talked about (chapter 22) and all that stuff about identity (chapters 28 through 38). Now that you can think in new ways, you're starting to figure out who you are, how you're different from others, and where you fit in. You're also becoming unique. Put a few five-year-olds in a room with some blocks, and it's easy for them to be instant friends. Sure, they have their differences, but not like you do with others at your age.

So here's the shift: Most childhood friendships are based on proximity—we live near each other or spend a bunch of time in the same place, so we've become friends. We know this isn't true for everyone reading this, but many (most?) of you can think back and remember when you were a little kid and your best friends were those who lived near you or spent a lot of time with you because your parents were friends.

But as you start to develop your identity, you start to base your friendships on affinity—"we like the same things." Sure, you might have friends who are totally different from you, but you'll usually find there's something you both enjoy doing or a common interest that provides glue to the friendship.

We're *not* saying you should hurry to dump your childhood friends. Seriously, a friend from childhood can be amazing. (We both still have friends—even as old as we are—who were our friends when we were kids.) We just want you to understand why you might be experiencing some change in your friendships. And that (again!) it's normal.

61. WHY ARE PEOPLE SO MEAN?

When someone yells at me, it can really bring me down. It's hard to understand, too, because it seems like it takes as much energy to be mean as it does to be nice. Why *are* some people so mean? Well, do you really want to know?

Here are a few reasons that *might* explain it. The crazy thing is that you can't *really* know why someone's acting a certain way, can you? But we've seen these reasons proven true so many times, they might explain at least *some* of the mean-ness you run into.

SOMETHING BAD HAPPENED.

Recently, I (Scott) met a guy who wasn't very friendly to me. Then I found out his one-year-old daughter had a really bad disease and *died* a few months ago. He said it feels like he's "walking around with a dagger in his heart, 24/7." Wow. I didn't know. But his story explains some things, doesn't it?

NOBODY'S BEEN NICE TO THIS PERSON FOR QUITE A WHILE.

It seems as if there's a lot of grumpiness going around, doesn't it? But when you're nice to someone first, that person's whole attitude can change.

This last reason is a little more difficult to understand—and a little more personal:

SOMETIMES PEOPLE WHO ARE CLOSE TO YOU ARE MEAN BECAUSE THEY'VE BEEN TRYING TO TELL YOU SOMETHING IN A KIND WAY, BUT YOU'VE IGNORED THEM.
Did you ever yell at your brother or sister because he or she *didn't* listen when you didn't raise your voice? It's kind of the same thing. Since the "mean" person really cares about you, it's possible she's trying to think of a way to "wake you up" to something that's true. Think about whether this person could be trying to *help* you, even though it doesn't *feel* very helpful. (Then maybe later you can ask her to help you in another way.)

HOW DO YOU *DEAL WITH* MEAN PEOPLE?
The best advice comes from the Bible. Check out Matthew 5:43-47 from *The Message* and replace *enemy* with *mean people*:

> *YOU'RE FAMILIAR WITH THE OLD WRITTEN LAW, "LOVE YOUR FRIEND," AND ITS UNWRITTEN COMPANION, "HATE YOUR ENEMY." I'M CHALLENGING THAT. I'M TELLING YOU TO LOVE YOUR ENEMIES. LET THEM BRING OUT THE BEST IN YOU, NOT THE WORST. WHEN SOMEONE GIVES YOU A HARD TIME, RESPOND WITH THE ENERGIES OF PRAYER, FOR THEN YOU ARE WORKING OUT OF YOUR TRUE SELVES, YOUR GOD-CREATED SELVES. THIS IS WHAT GOD DOES. HE GIVES HIS BEST—THE SUN TO WARM AND THE RAIN TO NOURISH—TO EVERYONE, REGARDLESS: THE GOOD AND BAD, THE NICE AND NASTY. IF ALL YOU DO IS LOVE THE LOVABLE, DO YOU EXPECT A BONUS? ANYBODY CAN DO THAT. IF YOU SIMPLY SAY HELLO TO THOSE WHO GREET YOU, DO YOU EXPECT A MEDAL? ANY RUN-OF-THE-MILL SINNER DOES THAT.*

Do you know any "mean people" who need your love?

I WAS A MIDDLE SCHOOL DORK!
—MARKO

This is one of the most embarrassing, humiliating moments of my young teenage years. It almost hurts to tell you about it. Please don't laugh at me.

Sixth-grade gym class. I'm not sure why, but our gym class was huge. There were like (I could be wrong on this) 50 to 75 kids in it. It was way larger than a normal class size.

The teacher's name was Mr. White. (I remember him clearly, even all these years later.)

On this particular day, we were having tug-of-war contests in the middle of the gym. You know, two teams pull on both ends of a massive, thick rope. I hated tug-of-war: It's all pull, pull, strain, pull. No movement. Just hurt yourself and pull harder. And get spanked in front of the entire class.

Wait, I jumped ahead.

We had various combinations of students taking each other on in a bunch of tug-of-war competitions—this group versus that group, on and on and on. And somehow, it was actually quite a bit of fun.

We non-tugging students were cheering on the sides—just yelling and whooping it up and making lots of noise—when, for whatever reason, I screamed a super-high-pitched scream, really loud.

I think I was just having fun, caught up in the excitement of it all.

Mr. White blew his whistle and stopped the tug-of-war match. When the class quieted down, he calmly asked, "Who's the screamer?" I knew he meant me, but I didn't see why it was a big deal—everyone had been yelling. I raised my hand.

Mr. White instructed me to walk to the equipment closet and get a paddleball paddle. (It's a large paddle made of wood—like a ping-pong paddle, but bigger.) I did as I was asked. Then Mr. White told me (remember, this was in front of the whole class) to bend over and hold my ankles. This isn't an easy thing to do, I should tell you. I was horrified, and then I started to realize what was happening.

And, sure enough, it happened. Right there in front of the entire gym class, Mr. White paddled me. (No teacher could get away with doing this today—he'd lose his job.) It hurt, and I cried, which made it 100 times worse. Mr. White just smiled—he didn't say anything.

I've often thought Mr. White was the worst teacher I ever had—if only for that experience.

DIFFERENCES BETWEEN GIRLS AND GUYS

62. WHY ARE GIRLS TALLER THAN GUYS?

My fourth-grade son just asked me (Marko) what I'm writing about, and I showed him the title to this chapter. When I told him the average middle school girl is taller than the average middle school boy, he said, "Really? Oh, man!"

The thing you've gotta keep in mind when it comes to your height is a message you've heard before (and, even if you're tired of it, here it is again): "Everybody's different."

Before puberty hits, you grow taller at an average rate of about two inches a year. Then sometime during puberty, you'll hit a "growth spurt"—a fantastic invention of God's that causes you to stretch out at a faster speed! But here's the crazy part: Even though the average man is taller than the average woman, the average *girl* hits her growth spurt *before* the average *guy*. (Did you like how many times I used the word *average* in that last sentence? Cuz everybody's different!)

If you're a guy, then that can be bummer news—especially if your growth spurt hasn't hit yet. You may not be too excited about the idea of looking up when you're talking to the girls in your class. And it might not be good news to you girls, either. It can feel awkward to tower above the guys, even if someone tells you, "Cheer up! Supermodels are tall." Yeah, but supermodels aren't in seventh grade, are they?

Here's some encouragement: Even though girls start shooting skyward sooner, a guy's growth spurt (when it finally arrives) usually lasts longer than it does in most girls. So by the time you're hitting late high school, it's all evening out. Usually. (We'd throw a "short" joke in here, but...nah.)

If you wish your height were different than it is, then you've got a great chance to embrace the fact that God made you the way he did *on purpose*! No mistake there. (Even though there are times we might wish God had made us six-feet-eleven-inches tall so we could play in the NBA.) Can you rise to the challenge of believing God knows what he's doing? It's all about getting comfortable with who you are.

I know a great guy named Joe who loved basketball, but his growth spurt was slow to arrive. What to do? He decided to go with it! During his freshman year of high school, when his buddies were already huge, he invited them to a "five-foot party" when he *finally* hit the milestone his friends had all blown past. Gotta embrace what you've got!

I also know a fantastic girl named Lindsey who was six feet tall in seventh grade. She says she really likes being tall—because that's what she is! Does she ever wish she were shorter? Maybe. I wish I were playing ball for the Chicago Bulls, but that's not happening, either!

63. WHY ARE GIRLS SO EMOTIONAL AND GUYS...NOT SO MUCH?

The first thing worth saying here is that not ALL girls are super-emotional and not ALL guys stuff or avoid expressing their emotions. So if you're a guy who shows his emotions easily—don't worry! It doesn't mean there's something wrong with you. In fact, it could be a good thing.

But...*in general*...a lot of girls are more *emotional* than guys are. And we're defining emotional as "openly expressing their feelings." So what's up with that?

Have you ever heard parents tell their sons, "Big boys don't cry"? A lot of guys start getting cues about how to handle their feelings while they're still pretty young. "Suck it up," "Deal with it," "Tough it out" are all phrases little boys hear. Little League coaches tell their players, "No tears—just rub some dirt on it." Somehow, expressing emotions can be seen as a weakness in guys. And in a world where strength and power and toughness are celebrated, showing your emotions can seem risky at best.

Another specialty of boys is that they often relate to each other by teasing or joking with their friends—much more than girls do. While lots of this is "just in fun," it doesn't make it feel very safe to share your feelings. Emotions can be uncomfortable; and when guys aren't comfortable, sometimes we handle it by joking and harassing each other instead of digging to see what someone's really feeling.

The funny part is that deep inside we ALL feel emotions sometimes. Positive emotions and negative ones. Because we're human, sometimes we're weak, sometimes we're scared, sometimes we're really, really sad. Nobody is strong and brave and fully in control 100 percent of the time. But there's a tough-guy part of us that sometimes wants to pretend we are. We "fake it." And when we fake it, we put ourselves in a really lonely place.

Guys, do you know anyone who won't laugh at you when you admit you're scared or sad or weak? That's a *real* friend. Talking with that person can be the beginning of getting comfortable with your emotions. And that'll really help you during middle school. Way more than rubbing dirt on it!

64. WHY DO GIRLS TALK SO MUCH AND GUYS...NOT SO MUCH?

If you're a girl, then you probably believe that some guys talk as often as a rock. And if you're a guy, you probably believe some girls are like a fire hose of words continually gushing syllables out of their mouths at an astonishing speed.

Of course, *all* girls don't use lots of words, and *all* guys aren't nearly wordless. But there *does* seem to be a pretty major difference between girls and guys in this area.

Researchers have studied this, and there's some pretty clear proof that the average teenage girl uses more words than the average teenage guy. Ready for some numbers that will blow you away?

THE AVERAGE TEENAGE GUY USES 3,000 WORDS A DAY. ASSUMING HE'S AWAKE FOR ABOUT 14 HOURS (LIKE, FROM 7 A.M. TO 9 P.M.), THAT'S ROUGHLY 214 WORDS AN HOUR, OR 3 1/2 WORDS A MINUTE.

THE AVERAGE TEENAGE GIRLS USES—READY FOR IT?—*20,000* WORDS A DAY. IF SHE'S AWAKE FOR 14 HOURS, THAT'S 1,429 WORDS AN HOUR, OR 24 WORDS A MINUTE, ALL DAY LONG!

Wow, right? That's a *big difference*. The average teenage girl uses almost seven times as many words as the average teenage boy. Dude!

There are lots of reasons for this; and, if researchers are honest, they'll admit they don't know all the reasons. They do know that girls' brains and guys' brains are somewhat different from each other. But even more so, they know that girls learn to process their thoughts with their words—to think about things by talking about them. Guys, on the other hand, learn to think about things in their heads, without talking very much.

Too much talking or too little talking isn't good or bad, really, although both can be annoying in the extreme. But sometimes it would be good for you, if you're a girl, to wait before speaking—think about what you're going to say. And sometimes it would be good for you, if you're a guy, to use words more often—not just grunts and other, um, noises.

65. ARE GIRLS REALLY MORE MATURE THAN GUYS?

Yes.

That's the short answer. (Sorry, guys.)

Okay, now for the longer answer. For some reason, girls go through puberty at a slightly younger age than boys do. Of course, as we said in chapter 10 (the chapter on puberty), there's a huge difference in when any young teenager—girl or guy—starts puberty. Some start as young as 10, some start as late as 14. Both ages are normal.

But on average (remember, *average* doesn't mean "right" or "better"—it just means "in the middle"), girls start puberty about one-and-a-half years earlier than boys do. This means that all the changes we've talked about in this book—the physical changes, the mental (brain) changes, the emotional changes, the spiritual changes, the relationship changes—they're all chugging into motion a bit earlier for girls than for guys. So girls basically get a head start on maturity.

Guys, this doesn't mean you're *not* mature. You'll catch up by the time you're in your late teenage years or early 20s. And this doesn't mean girls are *better* or *smarter* than you are, either. God just chose to give girls an early start on the changes that take place in the teenage years.

Let's ask God about it when we get to heaven someday, okay?

SECTION 9

QUESTIONS GIRLS
ASK ABOUT GUYS

66. WHY DO GUYS ACT SO STUPID?

Hey, are you calling us *stooooopid*?

When we don't understand something, we often call it "stupid." Just because we wouldn't do it that way, act that way, or talk that way, it seems stupid to us. But the truth is that maybe it's just *confusing* to us.

You already know that guys and girls are just so incredibly different. Believe it or not, God made us that way on purpose. And you'll probably spend the rest of your life trying to figure out WHY guys are so different from girls. (But it CAN be a lot of fun sometimes. Okay, and sometimes it makes us crazy, too!)

There are probably lots of ways girls think guys are weird and strange. Like, why are they so intrigued and amused by gross things? Boy, that's a tough one. I guess it's just how some boys are made. A herd of guys on the school playground might be huddled around a dead squirrel with its guts squashed out all over the place, or maybe they're checking out the oozing, bloody, drippy scab on their friend's knee. Girls say, "Gross!" But to guys, it's really cool.

Guys can also seem insensitive and rude. Why's that? Again, it's hard to be sure. Maybe it's because we're still learning. Lots of guys haven't figured out how to talk things out yet. Boys—in general—are more "action" oriented than "conversation" oriented. Back to that fourth-grade playground, you'll see more guys playing football or baseball or dodgeball or games that don't even involve a ball but still involve *action*. And while some girls enjoy playing those kinds of games, too, you're way more likely to see a group (or pair) of girls *just talking*, which can seem a little stupid to a guy. But guys, take note: Talking things out can help us avoid the insensitivity and rudeness we're sometimes guilty of.

Here's one more thing to think about—whether you're a guy or a girl—be careful how you judge people just because you don't understand them. Men and women, guys and girls—we're just different. And that's part of what makes relating to each other exciting. And crazy!

"WHY ARE GUYS SO WEIRD AND STUPID?"
—MORGAN, 7TH GRADE

CHANGES

67. HOW DO I KNOW IF A GUY LIKES ME?

BODY FACT: YOUR BODY USES 300 MUSCLES TO BALANCE ITSELF WHEN YOU'RE STANDING STILL.

He loves me, he loves me not, he loves me, he loves me not...

The "Does he like me?" question has been asked for a looooong time. And even today it's complicated.

In a word, it's about *attention*. Does he give you his attention? Then he likes you. Well...MAYBE he likes you. Of course, he might like you, but not *like*-like you. (We told you it wasn't simple!)

When a guy pays attention to you, it can be Good Attention or Bad Attention, right? It might seem obvious that a boy likes you if he comes and talks to you at your locker, writes you a note, or waits for you after school. Those behaviors could definitely mean he likes you. But even if he trips you in the hallway, steals your stuff when you're not looking, pulls your hair, or makes fun of the way you talk, well, that might *also* mean he likes you. Oh, boy!

In an earlier chapter, we talked about how guys often relate to each other by teasing or joking or making fun of their guy friends. So some guys figure that's also a great way to let a girl know they're interested in a friendship. They don't realize that calling you a nickname that makes fun of one of your physical features isn't your idea of friendship. (Be patient. It takes us a while to catch on to some things!)

In this book about changes, we keep talking about the different rates of change for different people. That rule applies here as well. Just because you're waking up to the thrill of guy-girl relationships, that doesn't mean the guy you're crushing on is in the same spot you are... not yet. If you like a guy, and it seems as if he's not returning your affection, then maybe he's just not thinking a lot about that yet. He might think you're a good friend, and he might even be a good guy to date in the future—but for now, his mind isn't on anything more that that. And you've gotta let that be okay! (BTW, make sure you read the next chapter.)

One other weird thing you should know about boys: Let's say you like him, and he likes you back. Then his friends get wind of it—and they start making fun of him all day long. (Hey, that's just how guys do friendship sometimes. You don't have to understand it, but you do need to know about it.) Well, the guy might defend himself by *swearing* he doesn't like you. Even if he *does* like you. Weird, I know.

We told you it was complicated!

So while guys are catching on to how the guy/girl friendship works, just be patient with 'em. They'll come around. Sooner or later. Or much later. Or much, much, much later.

68. *WHY* DOESN'T HE LIKE ME?

BODY FACT: THE AVERAGE COUGH COMES OUT OF YOUR MOUTH AT 60 MILES AN HOUR.

In the last chapter, we talked about how to know if a boy likes you. Maybe the only thing worse than not knowing is finding out he's not interested.

Before we talk about why that might be true, we need to be very direct about something else. *You can't make it "too important" if he's not into you!* Does that make sense? Yep, it might be a disappointment. It might even be a little embarrassing. But YOU are not defined by whether or not some guy likes you. You're way more than that! If you don't get anything else out of this chapter, then realize you're still fantastic—even if your dream dude isn't into you.

Okay, back to our question: *Why* doesn't he like me?

Well, it could be due to any number of reasons— or even no reason at all. Here are some thoughts:

MAYBE HE'S NOT READY TO "LIKE" ANYBODY YET.
Remember, girls tend to mature faster than guys. So it's possible he's not feeling the need for a girlfriend right now. And because saying that out loud could be embarrassing, he might be playing it cool.

MAYBE HE DOESN'T KNOW HOW HE'D ACT AROUND YOU.
When you're a middle school guy, you're still figuring out how you're supposed to "be" when you like a girl. Sounds funny, but it's true. And if you're not

sure...it's pretty risky to tell a girl you like her. That's a lotta pressure!

MAYBE HE'S JUST INTERESTED IN OTHER PEOPLE, TOO. He might not think you're a complete idiot; he might even think you're kinda cool. But maybe he simply just likes you for a friend—and that's it. (Someone might have told you that's just an excuse, but it's really not!) Having *friends* ("just friends") who are guys can be even better than the pressure of having a "boyfriend." Can you be okay with that? After all, the closest couples are great FRIENDS—they don't constantly have romantic, lovey-dovey moments like you see in the movies. So becoming a great *friend* will make you a super-great girlfriend—*when* the time is right.

We've gotta end back where we started: DON'T MAKE THIS TOO IMPORTANT! You're just figuring this stuff out—a few short years ago, you didn't even know much about it. Try to think about it this way: "If he doesn't like me, then it's *his* loss!" I think of all the guys who missed out on hanging out with my wife. But that means I'm THE ONE who gets to hang on to her forever!

69. WHY ARE GUYS SO OBSESSED WITH GIRLS' BODIES?

Okay—great question. If you're a girl, then you've probably wondered about this before, but maybe you've never gotten a guy's thoughts on it. And maybe "obsessed" is an exaggeration. But guys definitely seem to pay more attention to girls' bodies than the other way around. Let's see why.

THE AVERAGE GUY'S BRAIN IS SIMPLY WIRED TO BE VERY VISUAL IN NATURE—MORE *VISUAL* THAN THE AVERAGE WOMAN'S BRAIN.

What that means is that the stuff guys SEE impacts them differently than it does girls. It's really true! Smart scientist-types have scientific evidence that scientifically shows it, scientifically. Remember, it's a *general* rule because there is no "typical guy."

THE WORLD WE LIVE IN TAKES ADVANTAGE OF A GUY'S VISUAL NATURE.

Because a guy's brain is built to respond to what he SEES, people who want to get a guy's attention (like advertisers) know to use pictures, and it just reinforces a guy's visual viewpoint. Look around! Examples are all over the place. You see a billboard with a really attractive woman on it; but when you look closer, you see the billboard is selling—a watch. (BTW, the woman on the billboard isn't even wearing the watch. She's just there to get the guys' attention.) Think for a minute about how many ads try to grab a guy's attention by showing a woman. Advertisers do this because it works.

So what does this mean for girls? Another good question. First, although "showing more of your body" by wearing revealing clothes will probably attract some guys' attention, it's NOT the kind of attention you want. It probably won't get you attention from the kind of guy who's going to value you as a person. And it's *not* what you want to be known for. ("Hey, there goes the girl who wears skimpy clothes!")

And second, in a world crazed with appearances, don't overlook your heart. The Bible says that even when men are wrapped up in what can be seen, God is looking deeper:

> THE LORD DOES NOT LOOK AT THE THINGS HUMAN BEINGS LOOK AT.
> PEOPLE LOOK AT THE OUTWARD APPEARANCE,
> BUT THE LORD LOOKS AT THE HEART.
>
> —1 SAMUEL 16:7

God wants to grow WHO you are on the inside—*not* just what you look like. It's perfectly okay to want to look good, but when the outside appearance is the only thing you're paying attention to, you're going to come up way short of who God made you to be.

70. THE WEIRD STUFF TO TALK ABOUT: SPONTANEOUS ERECTIONS AND WET DREAMS

I can already hear some of you trying to hold back your giggles because of the title of this chapter. (We did that on purpose!) And some of you turned to this chapter as soon as you read it in the Table of Contents because you can't believe there's a chapter like this in the book.

We want to talk about it with you, cuz lots of people won't. And it's important information to know as you get older. Some people get really embarrassed by this kind of stuff, but honestly, they shouldn't. Everyone has a body, and it's important to know how it works.

Girls, these two things are simply part of a boy moving toward manhood—kind of like how getting your period is just part of becoming a woman.

Part of the maturing process includes your sexual parts. And as puberty hits, a guy's body starts to change.

Even though there are many slang words for it (yep—we've heard 'em all), an *erection* is simply when the tissue in a guy's penis fills up with blood, and the penis gets firm and stiff. An erection can be caused by sexual thoughts, BUT a guy can also get an erection *for no reason at all!* That's called a "spontaneous erection." Man, talk about awkward. But it happens...sometimes at the most embarrassing moments. Imagine having to stand up in front of the class when you have a spontaneous erection. Sounds hilarious—until it happens to *you*!

During puberty the body moves toward sexual maturity. As a guy's body changes, he'll often have a *nocturnal emission* (the official term), but it's also commonly known as a "wet dream." (See chapter 13; we covered it in more detail there.)

Whatever you do, remember that spontaneous erections and wet dreams are both very natural. They can be embarrassing, but they're not weird. It's just how a boy's body is made, and how it's getting ready to become a man. We don't know exactly why God designed people this way, but you've gotta admit—it's pretty creative!

Because these topics can make people feel awkward, people often don't know how to talk about them. We can't cover all this in a short chapter—but it's so important to talk about. We *really* encourage you to find an adult you trust and ask about these things. No, really! I can hear you thinking, *Are you crazy? That'd be major awkward!* And it probably would be. But feeling awkward and getting a straight story is way better than wondering and having questions that never get answered.

QUESTIONS GUYS ASK ABOUT GIRLS

71. WHY DO WOMEN GO TO SPECIAL DOCTORS?

When you're a boy, you pretty much go to the doctor only when you're sick or when you break an arm or a kneecap or something. Pretty straight up, pretty simple. But when you're a girl...

If you have an older sister, maybe you've noticed that she sometimes goes to the doctor when she's not sick at all. Some people call that person "the female doctor." That doesn't mean the doctor is always a female. It's just a doctor FOR females. Sometimes people whisper "female doctor" cuz they're embarrassed about it, but there's really nothing to be shy about.

During puberty some pretty big changes are taking place in a girl's reproductive organs (her uterus, vagina, and ovaries), and she'll also start her monthly period. You've probably talked about this in sex education classes at school. Basically, her body's getting ready to be able to have a baby, which means she needs some more mature equipment than she had when she was a little girl.

So a girl needs a special doctor (called a "gynecologist"—say GUY-no-college-ist) to deal with the health of her reproductive system. She needs to see her gynecologist regularly because her reproductive organs are more vulnerable to disease than guys' organs are, and she needs annual checkups. It's just a precaution to make sure she stays healthy for when (or if) she gets pregnant and needs to carry a baby inside her for 40 weeks.

One thing guys need to keep in mind is that this special doctor is a more "private" thing for girls. There's nothing embarrassing about it because it's a need for half the population (the girl half—get it?). But it's still *not* the kind of thing a girl wants announced in front of a whole bunch of people. SO, if your friend who's a girl mentions she has to leave school early to go to the doctor, your best move is NOT trying to impress your friends by shouting across the classroom, "SO...IS IT A GYNECOLOGY DOCTOR YOU'RE GOING TO SEE?" Not unless you want to get decked, that is.

And to have her not talk to you for the rest of the year.

And to get a visit from her big brothers in the middle of the night, with flaming arrows, attack dogs, and 50 rolls of toilet paper.

Okay, I'm exaggerating. But just don't make a big deal out of it.

72. WHY DO WOMEN HAVE TO CARRY A PURSE? AND WHY IS IT SO PRIVATE?

Ah, the private purse. Guys, have you ever tried to grab a girl's purse for a good old-fashioned game of keep-away? If you never have—don't try! Girls can get pretty possessive about that little bag.

So what's the big deal, anyway?

Well, first off, remember this: For some crazy reason, not all girls' clothes have handy pockets—like our jeans and shorts do. Pretty much anything we guys really need, we just cram into our pockets. (As a bonus, you can cram less-crucial items in your pockets, too, just in case you get bored and need some used gum, a bird foot you found, or an ear-bud that broke off an iPod.) But most girls' clothes aren't like that, which kind of forces them to drag a purse around. They don't seem to mind.

The average girl also seems to have more "stuff" to carry around with her than the average guy does. What stuff could be so important? Well, makeup, for instance. Whether it's lip gloss, eye shadow, or nail polish, some girls like to do "touch-ups" during the day. Or they just want to have it on hand to share with a girlfriend. Or they need it just in case they get thrown into a swimming pool. I don't know. Guys' lips and eyes and nails seem to do okay without any extra attention during the day. But then again, you've gotta admit that girls *are* way prettier than we are.

Now, this still doesn't explain the "private-ness" of that little bag, does it? Well, don't forget that girls have that monthly period to deal with. (And having you dig through her purse, pull out a tampon, and yell, "What's *this*?" is not her idea of a good time.) There are other reasons a girl's purse is sometimes more restricted than an FBI crime scene. She could also have love notes, money, her cell phone, a picture of her dog, and other stuff that's None of Our Business. Too bad!

Here's one more surprise: Sometimes girls carry a purse when they have absolutely nothing to carry in it. Nothing! They see purses as a "fashion accessory," something to make their outfits look better, like earrings or a necklace, we guess. And that's why so many girls have more than one purse.

Okay, this last one strikes us as kind of weird. Imagine having more than one wallet and switching the one you use based on what shirt you're wearing that day. Ha!

73. WHAT IS PMS?

Okay guys, this is a wild one. And we'll just tell you up front: It's one you may never fully understand, but it's definitely something you need to know about...and be sensitive about.

PMS stands for "Premenstrual Syndrome." Here's the scoop: When a woman is getting close to having her monthly period, the hormones in her body change. (Yep—every month.) And since we've talked a lot about hormones already, you know they can have an effect on so many things. With PMS, the effect is mostly emotional and physical...although, *it really is different for every girl*, and it can even be different from one month to the next—for the same girl. Not only that, but there are around 150 different symptoms that can be related to PMS. Not every woman has all of the symptoms, though.

Physically, PMS *can* cause headaches or make girls more tired than usual. It can also cause really painful cramps in their midsections or cause painful joints. It can even cause temporary weight gain.

Emotionally, PMS can make life feel like a roller coaster. A girl can feel depressed, grumpy, really anxious, or as if she wants to cry for no reason at all. It can be really frustrating for girls—especially in middle school. Like you, they're learning about and dealing with the changes going on in their bodies, too.

"Why don't they just take some medicine for it?" you might ask. Well, it's not that simple. Even with all the great medical wisdom we have, what causes PMS isn't completely understood. Sometimes the only thing that helps is good old-fashioned rest. When a girl misses a day of school, guys might ask her, "Were you sick?" and then feel really puzzled when she says, "Well...sort of." PMS is very different from the flu or the chicken pox.

We have a couple of tips for you guys:

BE UNDERSTANDING

Imagine dealing with something that's out of your control every month. You know it's coming, you know it's going to be uncomfortable and inconvenient (at best), and you know there's not much you can do about it. The last thing you'd want is some knucklehead making jokes about it or saying, "Don't worry about him—he must have PMS or something."

DON'T BE OFFENDED

When you're in a really bad mood, sometimes you say things you don't exactly mean. Girls who are dealing with PMS might do this, too. Don't take it personally. Then again, if you're joking around and harassing them, then maybe you *do* need to take it personally—and give 'em a break.

74. WHY DO GIRLS WHISPER AND GIGGLE SO MUCH?

What guy hasn't walked by a couple of girls, seen one of them lean toward the other one to whisper something, and then heard that silly giggling that seems to be a part of all Girl Language? Should you, as a guy, be embarrassed? Or should you feel complimented? Was it good? Terrible? You'll be glad to hear we have the answer for you:

You'll never know!

See, here's the thing about girls: Somewhere in the blueprints for all girls is wiring for chatting, talking, connecting, sharing secrets—and whispering. And that can be good. People weren't made to be alone. The first recorded problem in the Bible is when God said, "It is not good for the man to be alone" (Genesis 2:18). And while some guys can "connect" with each other by skateboarding or playing basketball for an hour and hardly saying a word—that's nearly impossible for girls to do.

Talking, whispering, and giggling—those are the ways of connection for most girls. And they might be "connecting" for lots of reasons, like maybe they're talking about how good-looking you are. ("Cute" is how they say it...as if you're a puppy or something.) Maybe they're talking about how one of them has a crush on you—or on your friend. Maybe they heard you aced the test yesterday, and they're talking about how smart you are. Or maybe you don't realize your fly is wide open!

Part of the reason girls whisper is because they don't want you to hear them. But there's another significant part to it: The feeling they get from being "in on a secret." You know the feeling. You hear a cool thing that not *everybody* knows, and you tell your buddy. The same is true with girls. Having a secret with someone kind of links you to that person. And when girls whisper and giggle, it gives them that same feeling.

One thing that's probably a waste of time? Trying to figure out *what* they're whispering about. That's the whole object of the game—keeping the information away from you. One strategy that might work is pretending you're not even interested in their *secret*. Most likely, any attention you give them will just increase their girl talk.

So the next time you hear the whispers and giggling, just smile and keep on walking. (Although it probably wouldn't hurt to look down and check your zipper, too!)

"GIRLS ARE ALWAYS GIGGLING AND WHISPERING TO EACH OTHER. I WONDER WHY."
—CHRISTIAN, 7TH GRADE

75. A FINAL REMINDER: YOU'RE GOING TO BE OKAY—CHANGE IS GOOD

Here we are at the end of the book already! Wow! We really hope you've had as much fun reading as we did writing.

This being our final page and all, we kinda feel a lot of pressure to say something super-important. So here it is:

Always wear clean underwear.

No, wait. That wasn't it. Let's try that again.

The one final thing we really want to make sure you know is—

Look both ways before crossing the street.

Oh, and eat your vegetables.

And don't take candy from strangers.

Stink! We're totally messing this up.

For real now, this is it. This is the one thing we want you to know about all the changes going on in your body and mind and emotions and relationships and faith and life:

YOU ROCK. YOU ARE TOTALLY AWESOME. WE DON'T CARE IF ANYONE ELSE THINKS THAT—OR EVEN IF YOU KNOW IT YET. BUT WE KNOW IT. AND EVEN MORE THAN US, GOD TOTALLY KNOWS IT. GOD COMPLETELY DIGS YOU AND LOVES YOU MORE THAN ANY OTHER KIND OF LOVE YOU CAN EVEN IMAGINE. AND IT'S PRETTY COOL TO HAVE THE CREATOR OF THE UNIVERSE AND THE INVENTOR OF YOU LOVE YOU THAT MUCH.

Bottom line, last sentence:

Not only will you be fantastic when you're done with all these changes we've been reading about, but you're also pretty wonderful right now.

There never seems to be enough time or money. Find the wisdom you need to help you use these resources to better your life and the world around you. As you explore the motivations behind how you use your time and money, the practical tips and biblical insights in this book will show you how you can manage these resources better.

Wisdom On...Time & Money
Mark Matlock
RETAIL $9.99
ISBN 978-0-310-27928-0

We all love a good song, movie, or TV show. But not everything out there is good for us. This book won't tell you what you should not listen to or watch. Instead, this book is filled with principles to help you gain the wisdom needed to help you make wise choices about what you choose to be entertained by.

Wisdom On...Music, Movies & Television
Mark Matlock
RETAIL $9.99
ISBN 978-0-310-27931-0

Visit www.invertbooks.com or your local bookstore.

If you've ever felt lonely, abandoned, lost, or unloved, you're not alone. Although she's a successful Gotee recording artist today, Stephanie Smith has had her fair share of hurt and heartbreak. Growing up fatherless, she struggled with her identity, self-esteem, and so much more. But today she's found hope in God that she believes can help you through your own heartaches and brokenness.

Crossroads
The Teenage Girl's Guide to Emotional Wounds
Stephanie Smith
RETAIL $9.99
ISBN 978-0-310-28550-2

Suddenly, it seems like everything in your life is changing. Your friends expect way too much from you. You fight with your parents more than you'd like. You just don't understand why your life seems so chaotic now. You are not alone. If you're feeling overwhelmed or confused with your life, this book will help you understand who you are, and give you hope for who you're becoming.

Mirrors & Maps
A Girl's Guide to Becoming a Teen
Melissa Trevathan and Sissy Goff
RETAIL $16.99
ISBN 978-0-310-27918-1

Visit www.invertbooks.com or your local bookstore.